This book is an omnibus edition of the author's other two books, with additional bonus recipes.

tw-eat – a little book with big feelings and short recipes for very busy lives

tw-eat more – a little book with more big feelings and short recipes for very busy lives

Published by Scarcroft Publishing

Printed by Ingram Spark

ISBN 978-1-7399670-0-0

tw-eat together

big feelings and short recipes
for those who cook & eat with love

@professor_dave

David K. Smith

Remembering Sam always

and with all my love to the 8yo

CONTENTS

TW-EATING TOGETHER

This book is an omnibus edition of my two cookbooks – *tw-eat* and *tw-eat more*. Together, these books tell the story of my family in an honest way through the food we cook and enjoy, alongside the love story between Sam & myself, the adoption of our wonderful, lively little boy, and Sam's untimely death leaving me as a single dad. I never thought so many people would be interested in our simple family recipes, the stories behind them, and the emotional resonance of what we eat. I want to thank everyone who has read and enjoyed those books from the bottom of my heart. I was overwhelmed when the *Guild of Food Writers* recognised *tw-eat* as 'Highly Commended' in their 2021 awards. Here, I wanted to collect all the recipes and stories together into a single luxury hardback edition – for good measure, I have added a handful of bonus recipes.

Highly Commended
Guild of Food Writers Awards 2021

"A touching portrait of fatherhood and bereavement...
tw-eat is much more than a collection of recipes"
Adoption Today Magazine

"Heartachingly beautiful"
"Simple tweet-length recipes"
"For those who cook and eat with love"
Amazon Reviews

My husband, Sam, loved good food and cooking. A famous family story told by his Mum, recalls the time that on a primary school trip to France, he was the only one of the kids who would try raw oysters – he ended up eating the lot. The last holiday we went on together was a night of luxury, and a fabulous meal, at Raymond Blanc's *Le Manoir aux Quat'Saisons* – visiting had been a life ambition of his. Even though he was almost too ill to walk from our room to the restaurant, when the beautiful plates of food arrived, his face lit up, and we talked animatedly into the small hours over many a glass of wine. Sam had cystic fibrosis, and when he eventually died aged 39, as a result of rejection of the lung transplant that had given him an extra 8 years of life, I was bereft. I was also a single dad to our then 6-year-old son.

Food had always been one of the threads that held us together as a family – we both loved to cook. From the time we first adopted our son, we had always shared family meals. Our food 'ground rules' were simple – we all tried new things together, only positive things would be said about food, and if something got left on the plate, so be it (there was always an extra slice of toast that could be found if someone needed to fill up later). Our son turned into an enthusiastic and adventurous eater. After Sam's death, food has been a vital thread that has helped us both keep going.

As well as being a single dad – a full time job in itself – I also work. I therefore needed simple recipes to easily feed myself and a hungry growing boy. Indeed, after becoming a widower, cooking was a sort of therapy for me. In addition, my son is at his most settled and happy when he sees me busy in the kitchen, cooking something (hopefully) delicious to eat, with him joining in where possible.

I started tweeting what I was cooking. First and foremost, I did this for myself, as a way of recording the things I had cooked that I thought were good, so that I could make them again. Partly it was to show my friends and family that yes, we were surviving, and I was managing to put food on the table. And partly it was a way of sharing the recipes, and in fact dinner, with my online friends. To tweet the recipes, I condensed them to 280 characters in a way that someone with modest cooking skills should be able to reproduce them.

I really wanted to collect together some of my favourite twitter-eats (tw-eats) into a book for easy reference. The things I cook are mostly simple – I have a busy life. However, my son and I have been through a lot – many of the recipes therefore deliver big in terms of comfort, and some are designed to look impressive for minimal effort. There are quick cooks and slow cooks, but in every case, they are briefly described in the form of a tweet. In just a few cases, I have broken a longer recipe down into two or three tweets, especially for some of the more special dishes towards the end of the book.

In general, unlike some of my original tweets, for the purposes of the book, I have tried to give precise quantities where needed - this may extend some recipes just a little beyond 280 characters - forgive me. In places where you can use your judgement, or personal preference, I have left quantities vaguer. The quantities are for 2 adults (or 1 adult and a very hungry 7yo, with seconds). Cooking temperatures are all for a fan oven - if you don't have fan, or have gas, add 20°C and convert. The recipes are very short, so I have dispensed with ingredient lists and just *italicised the ingredients* in the recipe itself - it should hopefully still be easy to make sure you have what you need.

I have added some extra words, partly to clarify things for the less confident cook or suggest tweaks and modifications to the recipes. Most importantly, however, I use these extra words to tell you our story, and what the food means to us. As recipes worm their way into the life of a family, they take on emotional resonance far beyond the simple combination of ingredients on the plate. This is what I really want to capture in this book - little recipes but big feelings.

During the Coronavirus crisis, as restaurants and coffee shops closed, I found myself cooking even more, and wanting to cook some of the things we might have previously gone out to enjoy. I think we have all become more interested in home-cooking, and food as therapy. At least I had a beautiful place to cook in. When Sam and I bought the house that was to be our forever home, the kitchen sold it to us - a large handsome room with a table at its heart. On becoming adoptive dads, and being joined by our special, caring, funny little boy, it became the focus of family life. All of us loved to spend time here - cooking drinking, talking, laughing. It's the room I live in. I wouldn't change it for the world.

At the heart of *tw-eat*, surrounded by simple recipes, is an exploration of the central role of Sunday lunch in the food culture of our family. This is something I brought from my own childhood, and gifted to Sam, who helped weave it into the fabric of our family life. At the heart of *tw-eat more* is a central exploration of outdoor food and the barbecue. My own family has no real culture of outdoor eating, but for Sam's family it's a huge thing – this is something he gifted to me. Now, just like Sunday lunch, it has become an integral part of our family's food culture. We might only have a small back yard, with a bit of artificial grass, but as soon as the sun is

out and the temperature rises above 18°C, we will be eating outside. I sometimes think that in our marriage, I brought the Sunday lunches while Sam brought the barbecues – I brought the comfort, he brought the sunshine. Together, they lie at the heart of this book.

In terms of work, I am a Professor of Chemistry. I manage a research team, teach students and am passionate about making science a more diverse & inclusive endeavour. Several people have asked me whether being a scientist was any influence on writing *tw-eat*. It is interesting to reflect that as scientists, we have years of training in writing accurate, but brief, experimental procedures, that can be replicated in laboratories anywhere in the world. In fact, this was the perfect training for creating simplified 'Twitter-style' recipes. In addition, synthetic chemistry is very like cooking in terms of the skills & techniques used in the lab. Indeed, if you want to see just how many chemists are passionate and talented cooks, just explore the Twitter hashtag *#chemistswhocook*. I have always said that my alternative career would have been as a chef. I really admire *Michael O'Hare* from *The Man Behind the Curtain* – one of my favourite restaurants. Just like him, when I lead my chemistry team, I help innovate and design the experiments (creating recipes), check things are done properly (kitchen management) and help my team present their achievements to the world (final dishes going into the restaurant). Putting this book together has been a joy and allowed me to indulge in my fantasy job.

One of the most amazing parts of publishing my two books, apart from the thrill of them being in print and holding a copy in my hand, was seeing people share what they have cooked from them – often copying me in *@professor_dave* or using the hashtag *#TwEat*. As a scientist, I am used to people 'citing' my research papers, but seeing people cook themselves nourishing and enjoyable meals from instructions I have published is intensely satisfying. It has been fascinating to see which recipes people choose to cook, how they change things to suit their families, and what emotions the food evokes in them. At the heart of the *tw-eat* books is the deep interlinking between food and emotions. The ability of food to capture a transient moment, give solace and comfort in dark times, or create family memories, is remarkable. So often, families end up in the situation where food is simply fuel. With the recipes and reflections in *tw-eat together*, I hope to show that food can be simple and fast to prepare, as demanded by family life, but can still be evocative, as well as delivering flavour and great comfort, and most importantly, bringing people together.

It is important to say I am just a cook, and this is just a collection. Many of the recipes were not designed by me – they are borrowed and adapted from the pages of my favourite cookbooks. I try to acknowledge these where relevant, but must highlight four of my muses: *Nigel Slater, Nigella Lawson, Diana Henry,* and *Harumi Kurihara.* I admire the fact that none of them are 'chefs' – they are all, first and foremost, writers, who happen to love food and cooking. As writers, and unlike many chefs, they are not scared to cut a corner, or do something simple, if it tastes good. They inspire me with their words and have done more to teach my family how to love food than I can ever express. In some cases, my only contribution is to strip back the elegance of their words into the form of a bare-bones tweet, tell you why I love the food and explain what it means to me and my family.

I hope you enjoy this collection. If not, at least I have created a family cookbook for me and the 8yo to use and treasure together, that we can both dip into, exploring the memories and food inspiration it holds within.

David Smith

SIMPLE SUPPERS – MEAT

CHORIZO and CHICKPEA STEW

 Fry 100g sliced *cured chorizo* in a dry pan until red oil runs out.

Add 2 sliced cloves *garlic*, chopped *onion*, fry.

Add 100ml *red wine*, reduce 50%.

Add can *chopped tomatoes*, *thyme*, simmer 20 min.

Add water if needed.

Add can drained *chickpeas*, simmer 10 min.

Serve with chopped *parsley*.

I first met Sam in 2006. Having known him for a little while (it's complicated – don't ask!), I finally asked him to become my boyfriend in a Spanish restaurant in Leeds. This dish takes me straight back there. In the years that followed, Spain also became one of our favourite places to visit. This simple stew is just the kind of thing you might hope to get in any good Spanish tapas bar. Scaled up like this, and served with lots of crusty bread, it makes a simple, but delicious supper. It's equally good with *butter beans* or *cannellini beans* instead of the chickpeas. It also makes a fantastic accompaniment to a simple piece of grilled, or pan-fried, white fish (see page 60).

PROFESSOR DAVE's STEAK FRITES

 Season *steak*, rub with *olive oil*.

Cook on hot griddle to liking, turn 90° halfway through each side. Rest.

Fry sliced *mushrooms* in butter, add generous *black pepper*, pinch *salt*, good shake *Worcester sauce*, 1tsp *Dijon mustard*, 50ml *single cream*, knob *butter* & juice from rested steak.

When I first met Sam, I could basically cook, but I didn't love it. It was Sam who loved food and cooking and fired my passion for it – sharing food with him was just the most fun you could have. Back in those earliest days, the first time he came to my house, I really wanted to impress him, so this is what I cooked. The secrets are simple. Choose ribeye if you want soft, buttery luxury steak, rump if you want more texture. Both have the best flavour - far better than sirloin or fillet. Season the steak well with salt and pepper - use a fancy salt if you want. Then cook it exactly how the other person wants it - cooking steak is an act of love. Fries should be deep fried, crisp & golden. I just stick frozen French fries in the deep fat fryer - buy the ones with the least possible coating on, naked if possible (the fries that is!). You then just need a really good sauce. Dinner in 10 minutes and Sam's heart won for ever.

SAFFRON & CHILLI GRILLED CHICKEN

Marinade 4 boneless *chicken thighs* in 4tbsp *olive oil*, juice of 1 *lemon*, 1 chopped *red chilli*, handful *mint*, 2 *garlic cloves* & large pinch *saffron*.

Cook on medium hot griddle, 8-10 min.

Serve with warm *couscous, preserved lemon, sultanas & parsley.*

Drizzle with *mint yoghurt, red chilli & mint.*

The first holiday I ever went on with Sam was to Morocco. The smell, taste and look of this dish remind me of walking round the night-time food market in Marrakesh, the 'Jemaa el Fna', and just wanting to eat everything. It was exotic, it was exciting. This dish is not quite the 'real Morocco', but it evokes it, and is really enjoyed by the 7yo, as long as I hold back a bit on the chilli. Thinking back to that holiday, we hired a 'car' (a story in itself) and drove south over the Atlas Mountains until the road essentially ran out, continuing on camels deep into the Sahara Desert where we slept under starlight. It was probably insanely risky for someone like Sam, with cystic fibrosis, but it was completely unforgettable, and honestly, if you don't grab those moments in life, what are you doing?

PORK TONKATSU

Bash *pork steaks*, dip in seasoned *flour*, then *egg*, then *panko breadcrumbs*.

Fry in 1cm *sunflower oil* until golden brown, 6-8 min.

Slice. Serve with boiled *rice* (optional: sprinkle *Shichimi Togarashi*), shredded *white cabbage* and *Bulldog Tonkatsu sauce*.

I adore Japan, and so did Sam – it has a unique marriage of vibrant modern pop culture and historical elegance. My ultimate Japanese comfort food is Pork Tonkatsu. Like Japan itself, it's a perfect marriage between 'in-your-face' crowd-pleasing crispy fried pork with sweet sticky sauce, and the cleansing, understated elegance of simple plain rice and crisp cool cabbage. I like it so much, I've even learned how to make my own Tonkatsu sauce for those emergency moments when I can't find any 'Bulldog' sauce. (Homemade *Tonkatsu Sauce*: 2tbsp *tomato ketchup*, 2tbsp *Worcester sauce*, 1tsp *soy sauce*, ½tsp *sugar*). I use a meat thermometer so the pork is perfect – although you will know as soon as you slice it.

I proposed to Sam in the evocative old wooden ryokan in Hakone that you can see in the photograph. We had a beautiful, elegant kaiseki dinner served to us in our room. Afterwards, we were sat just there, overlooking a babbling river, and I got down on one knee – the perfect marriage indeed.

CHICKEN YAKITORI

🐦 Glaze: 2tbsp *soy sauce*, 2tbsp *mirin*, 15g *caster sugar*, 1tbsp *sake* (or *dry sherry*). Heat & reduce until a bit thicker.

Thread cubed *chicken thigh* & *spring onion*, or *chicken liver* & *red pepper* on small skewers. Brush with glaze.

Grill/griddle until cooked, brushing glaze.

Serve with *lemon* & *mustard*.

👤 You must try this – the sweet, sticky glaze is a winner, especially with kids. Cut the chicken small so it cooks quickly, these are dainty skewers not kebabs. You can skip chicken liver, and just make all the yakitori with thigh if you prefer. Personally, my favourite is yakitori *chicken gizzards* or *hearts*; I love the chewy texture, but it's too hard to find them in the UK!

There are not many photos of Sam and I together, because I am usually the photographer. I love this one, taken by my best friend from college and the best man at my wedding, Jonny, who lives and works in Japan. The photo was taken when we were with him at a kushiyaki restaurant. We had a fabulous night out enjoying all sorts of food on sticks with dipping sauces before heading on to party in a Tokyo rock bar!

PARTRIDGE with BLACKBERRIES and JUNIPER

Mix crushed *juniper berries*, *butter*, *salt* & *pepper*, rub *partridge*, wrap with *streaky bacon*.

Roast, Fan 180, 20 min, remove bacon into roasting tin, roast 5-10 min more.

Peel and slice *parsnip*, fry in *oil*.

Mix steamed *cabbage* through *mash*.

Heat 50ml *port*, knob *butter*, handful *blackberries* & reduce.

Our butcher has amazing game in season, and partridge at the very start of the season is my absolute favourite – sweet, juicy, and delicious. Blackberries are also seasonal at the same time, so the marriage just seems perfect. This dish was always cooked at least once every Autumn when Sam was here – a seasonal ritual. Served with parsnip 'crisps' it becomes a special occasion quick meal (albeit unlike most recipes in the book, this is quite a hard-working 30 minutes). I'm assuming for the recipe you know how to make mash. The secrets are drying the *potatoes* in a hot pan after they've boiled to softness, putting them through a ricer for extra smoothness, and then being generous with *butter, milk, salt* & *pepper*.

YOUTUBER's LAMB and MINT CURRY

 Fry 1 *onion* in *sunflower oil* until brown, 15 min.

Add diced *leg of lamb*, brown.

Chop & add 2 cloves *garlic*, 15g *ginger*, 1 *green chilli*.

Add 2tsp *coriander,* 1tsp *turmeric,* 1tsp *cumin,* 1tsp *yellow mustard seeds, black pepper, salt,* fry 2 min.

Add ½ can *chopped tomatoes*, 200ml water, simmer 1 h.

Add 2 handfuls *peas*. Finish with chopped *mint.*

I have a YouTube chemistry channel – *professordaveatyork.* A long time ago, I cooked a lamb curry on video to explain some of the science behind curry spices. Although the chemistry was fine, the curry, in all honesty, wasn't very good. In the following years, I worked on the recipe, with Sam as a willing 'taster', and this is now my optimised version of a lamb and mint curry – taking the classic English combination and trying to make it work in a spiced setting. Leftover roast lamb is perfect for this if you have it, just add it later (after the spices) and drop the cooking time to 20-30 min.

ROAST CHICKEN and MAYO

Season *whole chicken* well with *salt, pepper & olive oil.*

Roast, Fan 180, 20 min per 500g + 20 min. Baste every 20 min.

Serve with warm *crusty bread, salted butter, dressed green salad* (*olive oil:balsamic vinegar*, 2:1) and *mayonnaise.*

Although it takes time to roast the chicken, the actual effort involved in making this is basically zero. It really is as simple as a ready meal. I know it sounds middle class and pompous but buy the best chicken you can – you really can taste the difference if a chicken has had a happier and more active life. It changes the quality of the meat – the legs are bigger and juicier, while the breast is less 'fluffy' and doesn't dry out the same.

This was Sam's favourite simple supper. Indeed, warm chicken and cool mayonnaise is a beautiful thing. Sam and I would sit across the table, carving bits off the chicken, drinking ice cold white wine, buttering bread, and talking, talking, talking... Now I kind of do it with the 7yo. He mostly talks to *Alexa* – she can tell good jokes – it's not the same, but it helps us both through.

SWEDISH MEATBALLS

🐦 Soak 50g *panko* in 75ml *milk*.

Soft-fry ½ fine-chopped *onion* in 10g *butter*. Add 1tsp *ground allspice*.

Mix 250g *minced beef*, 250g *minced pork*, ½ beaten *egg*, fried onion & soaked panko. Shape into meatballs.

Fry in *butter/oil* until brown, remove.

Heat 10g *butter*, ½tbsp *flour*, stir, slowly add 200ml *chicken stock*. Add 100g *sour cream*. Add meatballs, cover, simmer 15 min.

Serve on *mash* with *lingonberry jam* & chopped *dill*.

👤 Meatballs remind me of our honeymoon, which we spent exploring Scandinavia, travelling right up the Norwegian coast into the Arctic Circle, and then back down through Sweden. We were lucky to enjoy a heatwave in Stockholm and just loved the handsome Swedish capital, its equally handsome men, laid-back attitude, and meatballs. Of course, you can buy Swedish meatballs from *Ikea* – the 8yo loves them and they make a very quick tea, but these homemade meatballs, adapted from a *Diana Henry* recipe, are fab. You should, however, still get an *Ikea* jar of lingonberry jam – if you can't, just use *cranberry sauce* instead. This recipe makes enough meatballs for four, so you can freeze half of them after shaping them if there are just two of you.

QUAIL EGG, BLACK PUDDING and BEETROOT SALAD

Boil 6 *quail eggs*, 2 min 20 sec, peel and halve.

Fry chunks of *black pudding* in *oil*, 5 min.

Heat 25g *sugar*, 25ml *water*, *hazelnuts* until caramelised.

Cut *cooked beetroot* in wedges, add *mixed leaves*.

Dress: 2tbsp *olive oil*, 1tbsp *cider vinegar*, 1tbsp *honey*, 1tbsp *Dijon mustard*, *salt* & *pepper*.

Who says salads should be light? The 7yo is not the biggest fan of salads, but this is the kind of salad he will happily demolish. To be fair, it has everything you could possibly want - crunchy, soft, sweet, sour, earthy, rich. Ideal served with a hunk of warm bread, thickly spread with butter, at the end of a very bad day. Just be warned, never was so much pain hidden away so easily in four little letters, 'peel' - but it's worth it for the end result. If you can't get quail eggs, just use ordinary eggs and cut into wedges.

COFFEE-BRINED PORK CHOP

Make 500 ml *strong coffee*, add 15g *salt* & 3tbsp *dark sugar*.

Marinade 2 *pork chops* all day.

Dry.

Fry 8-10 minutes in *butter* & *oil*.

Serve with jacket *sweet potato* & *sweetcorn*. *Chilli butter* is good.

This doesn't necessarily sound promising – I wasn't that convinced coffee had a place in savoury cooking when I read the original *Diana Henry* recipe. But it turns out this is a real cowboy-inspired classic – make a big pot of coffee in the morning, pour the leftovers over the meat while you are out rounding up cattle. With the all-American sides of sweet potato and corn it just works and puts a smile on your face.

The first holiday Sam and I had after his successful lung transplant in 2011 took us out to the Western USA – Las Vegas, Monument Valley, The Grand Canyon and Death Valley. We made a spectacular road trip, feeling the freedom of the wide-open spaces and exploring the incredible National Parks and reservations. This recipe takes me straight back to that 'Wild West' landscape, made all the sweeter by the fact that when I first had this dish, Sam cooked it for me.

GRILLED SUMAC LAMB and PITTA CHIPS

 Marinate *lamb chops* in *garlic, olive oil, lemon juice, thyme.*

Soak thin-sliced *cucumber* in 25ml water, 25ml *white wine vinegar,* 1tbsp *caster sugar.*

Mix *yoghurt* & *mint.*

Put 7yo old to bed, 30 min.

Sprinkle chops with *sumac.* Griddle 3-4 min a side.

Slice *pitta bread*, deep fry 1 min, season.

Serve with extra *sumac.*

This is the kind of supper I make for myself when it's been a horrendous day, and I just want to get the 7yo into bed, relax with a glass of wine and escape into my Kindle (one of my most precious possessions). Lamb chops are perfect for this kind of cooking – they take no time to cook, but always manage to feel like an indulgent treat. It's also easy to get flavour into them very quickly. This recipe is simple, and the 'pitta chips' are a total revelation – maybe it's just the truth that you can deep fry anything and make it taste delicious!

PORK RAMEN

Heat 750ml *good stock*, sliced *ginger, spring onion, star anise*, 15 min.

Meanwhile, boil 2 *eggs* (8 min) & 'cook' *udon/ramen/rice noodles*.

Strain stock, add 1tbsp *soy sauce*, 1tbsp *miso paste*, 1tbsp *mirin*, 1tsp *sesame oil*, heat 5 min.

Add chopped *spring onion, spinach, sliced roast pork,* 1 min.

Add *cooked noodles*, top with halved *egg*.

One of the 7yo's favourite meals – every time we are in London, he wants to visit a very cool place in Soho for Ramen. Sam would have heartily approved. However, it must be said this specific recipe is only a simple supper – making proper ramen is a true, and time-consuming, art form, and this barely scratches the surface. This recipe is hugely versatile though – change the vegetables (*chard* or *beansprouts* are good), use different types of noodles, or omit the *miso paste* for a simple 'shoyu' (soy sauce) ramen.

One of my best memories from travelling in Japan with Sam was a day in Takayama when the rain was simply torrential. Having hiked round half the town and got thoroughly drenched, we found a tiny little place for ramen. Although the restaurant itself was humble, the steaming bowls of ramen were anything but – reviving and sustaining us in an almost magical way.

THAI-STYLE COCONUT LIME CHICKEN

 Marinade 300g diced *chicken breast* in juice & zest of 1 *lime*.

Fry in 1 tbsp *sunflower oil* & 1 tsp *sesame oil*, 5 min.

Slice and add 1 *green chilli*, 2 *spring onions*, 15g *ginger*, 2 min.

Add 200ml *coconut milk*, 1 tbsp *fish sauce*, 2 min.

Stir in chopped *coriander, basil, mint*.

Top with 2 *spring onions* cut in strips & more chopped *herbs*.

I was going to call this a Thai Green Curry – it has most of the components and spirit of it. However, given the amount of 'stick' I got on Twitter for my preference for a tiny splash of cream in spaghetti carbonara, I thought I would just call it Thai-Style Coconut Lime Chicken, so I didn't get accused of 'murdering' another classic! This dish is also great with less chicken and more veg – *baby sweetcorn* or halved *sugar snaps* are best. You can also replace the chicken with *mushrooms* and use *vegan fish sauce* to give a fragrant vegan dish. You don't need all three suggested herbs, you could just use coriander, but the combination is more 'Thai'. If you can get your hands on some *Thai basil*, then use that instead of the three herbs.

SLOW-ROAST SUMMER LAMB BELLY

Rub 3tbsp chopped *rosemary*, 2tbsp *yellow mustard seeds*, 1tbsp *garlic salt*, 2tbsp *celery seeds*, ½tbsp *thyme* leaves into 600g unrolled *lamb belly*, drizzle *olive oil*.

Roast wrapped in foil, Fan 150, 2 h, remove foil, Fan 180, 30 min.

Mix *asparagus* & sliced *red pepper*, *season*, drizzle *olive oil*, roast last 10-15 min.

Serve with thin mint relish (large handful chopped *mint*, ½ fine-chopped *shallot*, 2tsp *caster sugar*, juice ½ *lemon*, 1tbsp warm *water*)

You don't normally think of slow cooking as a summer activity, but in my opinion, this adapted slow-cooked lamb belly recipe from *Nigel Slater's* book *Eat* is surprisingly perfect for a sunny day. The secret to turning this dish into summer eating lies in how we usually serve it. I cut the lamb into strips that we eat with our fingers – dipping them into lemony mint relish along with roasted pepper slices and asparagus spears. If you need some carbs, then toasted flat bread (see page 212) also cut in strips is perfect, perhaps with some garlic butter. This is the way I loved to eat with Sam. We'd sit and chat about politics, life, friends, and family – dipping, eating, and talking – with a nice big glass of wine, his eyes sparkling as he put the world to rights.

TOAD IN THE HOLE

 Toad

Mix 1 cup (130g) *flour*, ½tsp *mustard powder*, 2 *eggs*, 1 cup *water/milk* (120ml of each), *salt & white pepper*.

Remove meat from *good sausages*, shape in balls, fry in *sunflower oil*.

Heat *sunflower oil* in baking dish, Fan 210.

Add browned meatballs, pour in batter. Bake, Fan 210, 30 min.

Gravy

Fry *sliced onion* & 1tsp *sugar* in 20g *butter* until golden, add 1tbsp *flour*, slowly add 400ml *beef stock*, stir.

I know Toad in the Hole (or 'Frog in a Bog' as we affectionately call it in our house) is a classic that anyone in the UK can rustle up, but that is partly the point of this book – it's an honest depiction of what we actually eat. Also, the 8yo absolutely loves this and will definitely want the recipe when he's older! When I was a child, my Mum used to make Toad in the Hole with slices of *corned beef* instead of sausages (that's not necessarily a recommendation). Rather than using whole sausages, we like the *Nigella* approach of shaping sausage-meat into bite-size balls. I have included a recipe for lovingly hand-made onion gravy, but in honesty, I often just fry onions until golden and put them in *Bisto* gravy – so don't feel any pressure!

CHICKEN and CAULIFLOWER CHEESE

🐦 In roasting dish: 4 *chicken thighs* (skin-on, bone-in), *cauliflower florets*, quartered *new potatoes*, halved *banana shallots*, sprigs of *thyme*, *olive oil*, *salt* & *pepper*.

Roast, Fan 180, 35 min.

Grate *parmesan* all over.

Roast for final 10 min.

👤 Traybakes are my favourite kind of cooking – just so easy. I mean honestly, why would you bother with shop-bought ready meals? This *Diana* Henry recipe is not the most colourful dish, but for comforting flavours on a winter's evening, it's hard to beat. This is the ideal kind of thing to cook on a school night and means I can help the 7yo do some reading or play a game while he waits. Alternatively, it just gives me a bit more time to clear up the trail of destruction he creates every time he gets home.

DUCK & APRICOT TACOS

 Season and prick 2 *duck legs*. Slow roast, Fan 150, 90 min.

Shred *duck legs*. Add to segments of ripe *apricots*.

Dress: 2 tbsp *olive oil*, 1 tbsp *lime juice*.

Finish with *coriander & red chilli* and serve on warm *tortillas*.

Ignore the oven for 90 minutes and then assemble something that is both beautiful and delicious – it's easier than one of those well-known branded tortilla kits. This recipe is totally compatible with being a single parent yet will make you feel like you're a million dollars. And what kids don't enjoy wraps? The apricots must be perfectly ripe, soft, and fragrant because they aren't getting any cooking. That makes this a delicious summer dish – as soon as you find perfect apricots, then go for it, you won't regret it!

PIGEON, BEETROOT and HAZELNUT SALAD

🐦 Prepare salad with blanched *mange tout*, chopped *cooked beetroot, cucumber, hazelnuts* and *crisp leaves*.

Dress: 2tbsp *olive oil*, 1tbsp *cider vinegar*, 1tbsp *honey*, 1tbsp *grain mustard*, *salt* & *pepper*

Season *pigeon breast*, fry in oil & butter, 2 min each side.

Slice & serve on dressed salad.

👤 Probably the most commonly-asked question on Twitter is 'How on earth do you get the 7yo to eat that?' Firstly, I'm lucky! He does genuinely love food. But secondly, we have always pushed his palate, while never making a fuss about food. Food has always been a big topic of conversation, and only ever talked about it in positive terms – what we like, how it tastes etc. I also carefully and strategically choose ingredients. In this case beetroot is one of his top favourites (I actively seek out beetroot recipes), mange tout and cucumber are also favourites of his, pigeon was new and he loved it, while the leaves and hazelnuts he didn't like and largely left (no fuss – we just try it together and talk about what it tastes like). Of course, a honey mustard dressing helps! There is then always some sort of fallback that he can fill up with – in this case lots of crusty bread.

BBQ CHIP-CHOS 1331

 Chop & fry 4 *spring onions*, 1 *red chilli*, left-over *roast chicken*.

Stir through 1 tbsp *BBQ sauce* & 50g grated *cheese* until melted.

Serve over *french fries*.

Add *sour cream, red chillies*, grated *cheese* & *BBQ sauce* to taste.

From a light, healthy pigeon salad, to sheer, filthy indulgence! There's a bar in York – 1331 – that invented 'chip-chos'. Essentially, they are Nachos, but with the tortilla chips replaced by french fries. In 1331, they come with all the traditional Mexican toppings – beef chilli, guacamole, salsa, sour cream, cheese (do try it, it's great). I decided to take the idea in a spicy barbecue direction as a way of using up some leftover roast chicken. It's phenomenal!

1331 is a very special place for us as a family. You can hire the upstairs rooms for private parties, and it has marked some of the key points in our lives. When we formally adopted the 7yo, we had the celebration party there – they even have a mini-cinema, where we played cartoons for all the kids (and some of the grown-ups) to watch. When we scattered some of Sam's ashes at his memorial bench in Museum Gardens, it's where friends and family went afterwards for a drink and a chat. Irrespective of the occasion, we always make sure there's a big pile of chip-chos!

ICELANDIC LAMB CHOPS

🐦 Cube *potatoes*, *season*, toss in *olive oil*. Roast, Fan 180, 30-40 min, toss/turn halfway through.

Roast *red pepper* in olive oil. Fan 180, 20-30 min. Remove skin, mash with *feta*, a trickle of olive oil & a squeeze *lemon* juice.

Season *lamb chops* with *Icelandic lava salt & pepper*. Griddle, 3-4 min a side. Render fat by holding fatty edge directly on griddle pan.

👤 We had a wonderful family holiday in Iceland. One meal really sticks in the memory. After a long day exploring the magical glaciers & ice fields of Eastern Iceland, we returned to the farmstead where we were staying, and they served us their own lamb. It was simply done, but absolutely delicious. Here, I seasoned the lamb with Icelandic 'lava salt' to help evoke the memory, but any good salt will do. Vegetables are often imported in Iceland, so I don't feel guilty about serving the lamb up with Greek-style roasted red peppers. The 'parmentier potatoes' are a mainstay in our house. They are a super-easy side dish with minimal effort, delivering crunchy, crispy, roasty, toasty edges and soft insides. They can be further improved by adding rosemary or a clove of garlic.

'JERUSALEM' CHICKEN

 Peel & quarter *Jerusalem artichokes*. Boil in water with a squeeze *lemon juice*, 10 min. Drain.

Add to 4 *chicken thighs*, 6 halved *shallots*, 3 cloves sliced *garlic*, 1 sliced *lemon*, 2tsp *crushed pink peppercorns*, big pinch *saffron*, *thyme*, *tarragon*, *salt*, 3tbsp *olive oil*, 2tbsp *water*.

Marinade as long as you can.

Roast, Fan 180, 45 min.

I adore this dish and the 7yo just about tolerates it – in honesty, Jerusalem artichokes are at the very limit of what I can serve him, although he is always more tempted to try them when I tell him they make you fart. It's a very easy traybake, prepared with minimum effort and tastes amazing. The recipe is adapted from *Yotam Ottolenghi*'s Jerusalem cookbook. Every February, when Jerusalem artichokes come into season, and there is so little other good local seasonal produce, I just have to cook it. I serve this dish with a good sourdough bread, so the 7yo has plenty to fill up with.

GAMMON and PINEAPPLE SALSA

Cook *gammon steaks* on hot griddle, 3 min each side.

Mix ½ chopped *fresh pineapple*, ¼ chopped *red onion*, ½ chopped *red chilli*, juice of 1 *lime*, small handful chopped *coriander*.

Serve with *french fries* and possibly a *fried egg*.

Considering Sam lived all his life with cystic fibrosis and knew that ultimately his life would be limited by it, he had an incredible positive mental attitude. His ability to look to the future in an optimistic way was a massive influence on me and is something I try to pass on to the 8yo. Sam very rarely got fed up, and if he did, it was usually about relatively trivial things, like frustration with me because I hadn't helped enough around the house. On the rare occasions Sam did feel genuinely low, gammon and pineapple was one of his go-to dinners. My contribution to his tradition was to persuade him to make a simple pineapple salsa to go with the gammon. The heat of the chillies and the acidity of the lime perk up the dish and help lift the lowest of spirits.

DUCK and CANNELINI BEANS

🐦 Season & slash *duck breast.*

Fry in dry pan, medium heat skin side down, 5 min. Flip, 1 min.

Drain can *cannellini beans*, place in small roasting dish with *rosemary* & glug of *dry marsala wine.*

Put duck on top, breast side up. Roast, Fan 180, 15 min.

Partly mash the *cannellini beans* & serve.

👤 Duck breast makes a very fast supper and is one of my go-to meals after a hard day, when I decide I want to eat on my own, with the 7yo tucked up in bed, just to de-stress. This way of cooking duck breast (5 min in pan, 15 min in oven) is a bomb-proof way of getting pink juicy delicious meat and perfect crisp skin, turning it into a real hero ingredient. I also like to serve duck breast on *lentils* (whisper it quietly – I quite like microwaveable packets of ready-prepared flavoured lentils as a simple base for a duck breast). A glass of Pinot Noir is an essential accompaniment – just make sure you haven't already drunk too much of the bottle beforehand while de-stressing.

DUCK LEG with SWEET & SOUR CRANBERRIES

Season and prick *duck leg*. Roast, Fan 150, 90 min.

Cube *potatoes*, season, toss in *sunflower oil*. Roast, Fan 150, 60 min.

Take 25g dried *cranberries*, 100ml *red wine*, 1 tbsp *red wine vinegar*, 2tsp *sugar*. Simmer & reduce to a sticky sauce.

Use good *salad dressing* (I buy Mary Berry's 'Classic') on *leaves*.

An easy luxurious supper that I sometimes have if the 7yo is away at his grandparents and have some time to myself. I will be catching up on my favourite podcasts (my kitchen is strictly a TV-free zone), and relaxing. Other than opening and closing an oven door, mixing a few things in a pan, and leaving to simmer, there really is nothing to it. In this case, because the 'parmentier potatoes' are cooked alongside the duck they are at a lower temperature than those on page 31, so they get longer in the oven. The dressed leaves here were *lamb's lettuce* – I love their mild softness. If you wanted something with more character, then *watercress* dressed in *olive oil* and *balsamic vinegar* would be fantastic and add a touch of bitterness to counteract the sweet & sour sauce.

ITALIAN MEATBALL & FENNEL SPAGHETTI

Take *Italian fennel sausage* out of casings, make into meatballs, fry till brown.

Fine dice *fennel & onion*, fry till soft. Add *garlic*.

Add ½ can *chopped tomatoes*, meatballs & splash *red wine*.

Cook 15 min.

Serve through cooked *spaghetti* with *parmesan*.

We are lucky that on our local high street, the award-winning 'Bishy Road' there's an amazing Sicilian café, and even luckier that the owner, Beppe, sells sausages made to his mother's recipe. Beppe has always been a good friend to Sam, me and the 7yo – he currently chairs the Bishy Road Traders' Association and embodies the true meaning of local community. His sausages are a 'hero ingredient' and can elevate any dish to the next level. Buy some of his amazing ice cream while you are there, and you can do the same to pudding (see page 182). You are then ideally placed to create one of the simplest, but tastiest two-course meals you will ever cook.

GNOCCHI with STEAK and ASPARAGUS

🐦 Boil ready-made *gnocchi*, 1-2 min.

Boil/steam *asparagus*, 2-3 min

Fry *steak* rare. Rest.

Add gnocchi & a knob of *butter* to steak juices in pan, fry 3 min.

Make dressing: 3tbsp *olive oil*, 1½ tbsp *lemon juice,* chopped *basil*, grated *parmesan*, ½ clove chopped *garlic*.

Plate gnocchi. Add sliced steak & asparagus. Dress.

👤 There are days when you just want a taste of luxury but don't want to make any effort. This takes 10 minutes from start to finish and with two luxury ingredients on the one plate feels like a real treat (you can make one good-sized steak stretch between two people). I had a version of this on the day they announced that the first Coronavirus vaccine looked like it worked! Frying the gnocchi in the juices in the steak pan is not essential, but it really takes the dish to the next level as they soak up all that flavour and get a toasty, crisp golden exterior.

CHICKEN & BASIL TRAYBAKE

 Cut *potato* to 2cm dice.

Place in roasting tin with *chicken leg pieces* (bone in, skin on) and 2 squashed cloves *garlic*. Season with *salt* & *pepper* (especially chicken).

Toss in *olive oil*, squeeze half *lemon* over, throw squeezed lemon half in tin.

Roast, Fan 190, 30 min. Add *basil*, roast 10 min more.

Remove chicken & potatoes. Add 100ml *white wine*, reduce on hob.

Serve with roasting juices, *green salad* & more *basil* leaves.

A traybake – one of the easiest forms of cooking, yet utterly delicious. The 8yo loves it when I serve chicken on the bone, because he gets permission to eat using his fingers! This dish has all the flavour of roasted chicken, fragrant garlic, herbs & lemon, with chip-like potatoes, but only needs 40 minutes cooking and 10 minutes of actual effort. Even better, using the splash of white wine to enhance the pan juices is the perfect excuse to open a cold bottle of your favourite tipple and make sure you have a very large glass of it with your dinner. It's perfect food for a summer afternoon in the garden.

ORECCHIETTE, BACON, COURGETTE & PECORINO

 Cook 200g *orecchiette pasta.*

Fry 100g chopped *bacon*, 3 min.

Finely chop & add 1 small *courgette*, 1 *shallot*, 1 clove *garlic*, 5 min.

Add ca. 50ml *double cream*, heat.

Add cooked pasta, generously grate *pecorino cheese* over.

A simple, tasty pasta dish. Make the sauce while you cook the pasta, and you will have dinner on the table in 15 minutes. Obviously, Italians might use *pancetta*, but bacon is fine. For the pasta, you want something small and 'open'. Orecchiette are perfect and are one of my favourite pasta shapes for eating, but conchiglie or farfalle would work fine. In honesty, you can use whatever cheese you like – when checking my original tweet, I used Spanish *manchego*, and it was delicious (shhh – don't tell any Italians). However, for the purposes of the recipe, I have suggested a more conventional Italian cheese. If you haven't used *pecorino* before and always go for *parmesan*, it's worth giving it a try. As a sheep's cheese it has a cleaner, sharper taste, and goes particularly well with simple, light, vegetable-driven pasta sauces.

SHEPHERD's PIE

Finely chop 1 *onion*, 1 *carrot*, 1 *celery* stick and gently fry in *olive oil*. Remove.

Brown 450g *lamb mince*, adding ½tsp *cinnamon*, *salt* & *pepper*.

Add 1tbsp *plain flour*, stir. Add veg, 275ml *vegetable stock*, 1tbsp *tomato puree* & 1tsp *thyme* leaves. Simmer, lid on, 30 min.

Put in baking dish. Top with loosely-riced *mashed potato*, drizzle with 25g melted *butter*, scatter 50g *cheddar*.

Bake, Fan 180, 25 min.

This Shepherd's Pie recipe is classic British family cooking comfort food. It's adapted from *Delia Smith*, but by keeping the mashed potato topping loosely riced and drizzling with butter, the top goes deliciously crisp as it bakes. The recipe is enough for four people - you can make half quantities, but rather like lasagne, it somehow doesn't feel right to make a small Shepherd's Pie. You can reheat leftover portions in the microwave. I might be crazy, but I think that (rather like a Lancashire Hotpot) Shepherd's Pie goes really well with *pickled red cabbage* - the acidity helps balance out the richness of the lamb, but you can always be more traditional and serve *peas*.

STU's HEALING ITALIAN CHICKEN MEATBALL PASTA

🐦 Take *Italian chicken sausages* ('Chicken Italia', *Heck*) out of skins and form small meatballs (or simply cut the sausages into pieces).

Fry in *olive oil* till brown, remove.

Gently fry fine-diced *onion/carrot/celery* till soft. Add chopped *garlic*.

Add *can tomatoes, Italian herbs*, chicken meatballs, *black olives*.

Cook through, season, add to *pasta*.

👤 In Sam's final days, when his transplanted lungs were rejecting, after the 8 fantastic years of extra life they had given him, he was hospitalised on the cystic fibrosis ward in Leeds. The ward is amazing, with caring and dedicated staff who really understand CF patients and their families. They essentially let me live on a sofa bed in his hospital room. Probably the best thing I ate in the month I spent there was brought in by Sam's brother, Stuart. It was a simple pasta dish in a Tupperware container that I could microwave-up in the ward kitchen. After endless days of ready meals and Costa sandwiches it tasted great – real soul food. I have cooked it often since and thought of the comfort it brought me in such a difficult time.

CHICKEN and MUSHROOM PIE

Fry generous (ca. 250g) sliced *mushrooms* until reduced.

Chop *leftover roast chicken*.

Melt 25g *butter*, add 25g *flour*, 250ml *chicken stock*, 50ml *milk*, *salt & pepper*.

Place ingredients in 20cm pie tin, pour white sauce over.

Top with *puff pastry*, trim, decorate. Brush with beaten *egg*.

Bake, Fan 180, 30 min.

After a roast chicken (pages 18 & 170), I often make a chicken pie to use up the leftovers (with *chicken stock* made from the carcass – let it simmer for an evening with *bay leaf, parsley stalks, 2 peppercorns, ½ onion* and *carrot*). I prefer the pie with mushrooms, but *sweetcorn* is also good (just open a can, drain, and tip it in). If you are feeling more ambitious, make your own *shortcrust pastry* (rub 110g *flour*, 25g *lard*, 25g *butter*, & *salt*; add 1-2 tbsp *water*, leave 30 min in fridge, roll). I always used to decorate the top of the pie with a message, but for some reason stopped, and forgot all about it. Then one day, the 7yo said 'You never put messages on your pies anymore – is it because Pop died?'. So, I made him this pie specially. Pies are always made with love, but I think they taste even better when they say it on the top!

CHICKEN and CHICKPEA MADRAS PIE

 Chop 1 *onion*, 1 clove *garlic*, 15g *ginger*.

Gently fry *onion* until soft, then add *garlic*, *ginger* and 1 tbsp *Madras curry powder* and fry 2 min more.

Add chopped *roast chicken*, drained can *chickpeas*, place in pie tin.

Make *white sauce* and pour over as on previous page.

Finish pie as before.

A simple, tasty, slightly crazy, very basic 'East meets West' adaptation of the standard pie recipe on the previous page and a gateway dish designed to get the 7yo interested in eating Indian food. I grew up as a huge fan of Stockport County, going to Friday night matches with my dad. Nowadays, the Balti Pie is a staple at football grounds across the North West – consider this a home-made homage to the mighty 'boys in blue' (sadly now somewhere close to the bottom of the football pyramid). Serve with buttered steamed cabbage that has caraway seeds stirred through at the end and maybe some naan bread to mop up the Madras-spiced sauce.

JAPANESE MISO MARINADE STEAK FRITES

 Marinade *steak* for 2-3 h in 2tbsp *miso*, 1tsp *soy sauce*, 2tsp *mirin*, 2tsp *sake* (or *dry sherry*).

Drizzle steak with *olive oil*. Cook on hot griddle to liking, turn 90° halfway through each side. Rest.

Dressing for shredded *little gem lettuce*: 1tbsp *olive oil*, 2tsp *rice wine vinegar*, 1tsp *sesame oil*, 1tsp *soy sauce*, sprinkle of *shichimi togarashi* (or *black pepper*).

Serve with *fries* and *wasabi*.

This is a great Japanese twist on steak frites, inspired by *Harumi Kurihara's* double miso steak recipe. The steak takes on a deep umami miso flavour. The wasabi perfectly plays the role that mustard or horseradish would have in the Western version. It's worth noting the steak will char on the griddle slightly more quickly than a normal steak because of the sugar in the mirin. The Asian dressing for the lettuce is wholly my invention. If you can't find *shichimi togarashi*, the best alternative is scant crushed *red chilli flakes* and ground *sesame seed*, but *black pepper* will do. If you want to be healthier, replace the fries with simple steamed rice. It's an indulgent luxury steak supper to impress your loved one – or just make yourself really happy.

PORK, MUSHROOMS, GINGER, KIMCHI

🐦 Fry 200g sliced *pork steak* in hot *sunflower oil*, 2 min.

Add 15g sliced *ginger* & 200g quartered *mushrooms*, 2 min.

Add 1tbsp *soy sauce*, 1tbsp *mirin*, 100g *kimchi*, 1 min.

Add 1tbsp *rice vinegar* & 2 sliced *spring onions*.

Serve with steamed *jasmine rice*.

👤 This fusion of Chinese and Korean food is a super tasty, very fast stir-fry dish. The kimchi is the star here, lifting an average stir fry into something special. I was unsure whether the 8yo would eat kimchi, but in fact, he loved the umami flavours and slight spice this dish delivers, and it was very quickly demolished. It would be easy to produce a flavour-packed vegan version of this dish by replacing the pork with *shiitake mushrooms*. I serve this with plain jasmine rice. The 8yo adores plain rice, and since I got a rice cooker, which makes perfect rice every time with no effort, I have even found myself really enjoying its simple pleasures. However, this would also be great with *egg fried rice*, and I know some kids would prefer that. (In brief: Very quickly stir fry 1 *egg* in *oil*. Add *steamed rice* that has been chilled in the fridge. Add 1tbsp *soy sauce*, handful *peas* and chopped *spring onions*. Fry till rice gets crisp fried bits).

PORK STEAK with DIY SAUCE

Bash *pork steaks*, coat in *seasoned flour*.

Fry in *butter/oil* (ca. 3 min per side), remove.

For cream sauce: Add 100ml *white wine*, reduce 50% scraping pan. Add 10g *butter*, 100ml *double cream*, pinch *salt*. Flavourings (choose from): *Dijon mustard, grain mustard, lemon* juice, *green peppercorns, tarragon, parsley*.

For lemon butter sauce: Add 100ml *white wine*, reduce 50% scraping pan. Add 25g *butter*, juice of half a *lemon*. Flavourings (choose from): *tarragon, parsley, sage, thyme, capers*.

This is tasty and versatile, guaranteed to get your dinner on the table in 10 minutes. Once you have perfectly fried your pork steak, you then only need to decide what sauce you want to serve it with. The photograph shows a mustard & green peppercorn cream sauce, which is delicious, but as the recipe explains, you can easily select the sauce to make the dish suit your mood. Whatever you choose, the sauce will take up all the savour of the pork from the frying pan. To get it on the table, serve with deep-fried french fries (or bread), and some simple boiled vegetables (or side salad). With all the possible variation here, your family won't even notice you're essentially just cooking the same thing.

SLOW-COOKED LAMB & BLACK OLIVE TAGLIATELLLE

🐦 Gently fry 1 chopped *onion* in *butter* & *olive oil*.

Add chopped *garlic clove*, 350g *diced lamb shoulder*, 50g chopped *black olives*.

Add 100ml *white wine*, reduce 50%. Then add 250ml *chicken stock*.

Simmer 2 h, top with water (or Fan 140, 2-3 h, or slow cooker, 6 h).

Reduce. Add 200g cooked *tagliatelle*, finish with chopped *parsley*.

👤 This is not a typical quick-cook pasta dish – but it doesn't take much work. Adapted from a *John Whaite* recipe, it delivers a massive smack of umami thanks to the black olives and qualifies as real comfort food. Ideally, put this in a slow cooker (or low oven) once you get to the 'long simmer'. You can then leave it with a lid on and head out for a long wintry walk. When you get back home into the warmth, all you need do is boil some pasta, reduce the sauce, and a super-satisfying supper is done. Me and the 8yo both love getting out in nature – these last few difficult years, it has helped to keep us both sane. This is just what I want to eat when we get home.

CHICKEN KARI KARI

Prick skin on 3-4 *chicken thighs*, add *salt & pepper*.

Fry in *sunflower oil* skin-side down until golden.

Turn over, cover with a circle of tin foil, turn heat down, cook through.

Slice and top with a mountain of chopped *chives*

Serves two with *rice, mustard, pickles* and *ponzu soy* dip.

Crowd-pleasing Japanese food in minutes! You can buy *ponzu* in supermarkets now, but if you can't find any, just mix *lemon juice* and *soy sauce* in roughly equal quantities. As you will see throughout this book, we adore everything about Japan, the country we loved to visit and where I proposed. Indeed, Sam and I had a loose Japanese theme at our civil partnership. Although the food on our big day wasn't Japanese (we wished it could have been), we decorated the tables with bonsai trees and folded well over a thousand tiny origami cranes to bring us the best possible luck and happiness. I like to think all of that folding helped secure Sam his successful lung transplant just 6 months later. Looking ahead to the future, I can't wait to take the 8yo to Japan – given how enthusiastically he demolishes the food, he's going to love it!!

SPAGHETTI al RAGU

 Finely dice 1 *onion*, 1 *carrot*, 1 *celery stalk*. Gently fry in *olive oil*. Remove.

Fry 3 chopped rashers of *unsmoked streaky bacon* and 450g *minced beef* – as it browns, season with *salt, pepper* & 2tsp *dried Italian herbs*.

Add 1 glass *red wine*, reduce 50%.

Add cooked veg, *bay leaf*, 400g can *chopped tomatoes*, ½ can *water*.

Simmer 1-2 h, add water as needed. Serve through cooked *pasta*.

The 8yo adores Spaghetti Bolognese, so there's almost always some of this sauce in the freezer. I cook a batch for 4 people based on the recipe above and freeze the leftovers. Don't pile the sauce up on top of the pasta (it's supposed to coat it), don't use too much sauce, and don't ever ask for 'Spaghetti Bolognese' in Italy, it's not authentic – although they have pasta 'al ragu', which is something similar on *tagliatelle* or *pappardelle*. The photo shows the last physical meal Sam ever cooked for me. It was a few months after he died when I pulled this batch of 'Bolognese' sauce from the freezer – he had made it before he passed away. Knowing how important food was to him, and that he had chopped, stirred, seasoned & tasted it, made for a very special, but sadly reflective moment.

SIMPLE SUPPERS – FISH

MOULES MARINIERE

Clean *fresh mussels*, discard broken ones or ones that stay open if tapped.

Chop 2 *shallots* & 1 clove *garlic*, gently fry in *butter* in large pan.

Add mussels, 100ml *white wine*, put lid on.

Cook 4-5 min until mussels open.

Add 100ml *double cream*.

Finish with chopped *parsley*.

Like father like son – my boys absolutely love(d) mussels. Hands-on, fingers-messy eating, it's surprisingly perfect for kids and a good way for encouraging children to become more adventurous eaters. If they don't like the mussels, they just fill up on bread and butter, dipping it in the creamy 'soup'! I love these two photos of Sam and the 7yo, taken almost 30 years apart. When I'm particularly exhausted at the end of a long day, I have been known to do 'Boil in the Bag' Moules Mariniere from a well-known supermarket. They are not quite as good as the real thing, but they still hit the spot for the 7yo.

COD TRICOLORE

 Place 2 *cod fillets* in roasting tray with halved *cherry tomatoes*, *basil* leaves, torn *mozzarella*.

Season, grate *parmesan* over, drizzle with *olive oil*.

Bake, Fan 180, 15 min.

Serve with cubed *rosemary roast potatoes* (see page 31).

Traybakes are a fantastic way to introduce kids to cooking. Why are we Brits so obsessed with teaching kids to bake cakes? They are not very healthy and it's not the best cooking life skill (unless you want to win the 'Bake Off'). There is just as much pride (if not more) to be gained by children in cooking the dinner you are going to sit down and eat together. This is so quick and simple, looks beautiful, and the 7yo loves to steal some of the uncooked mozzarella and cherry tomatoes as he prepares it. The recipe is adapted from *Jamie Oliver* – I really admire the way he's done so much to revolutionise British food culture.

CLAM CHOWDER

🐦 Finely-dice & gently fry ½ *fennel*, ½ *onion*, ½ *leek*, 3 rashers *bacon*.

Add 150ml *white wine*, reduce 50%.

Add 1 litre *fish stock*, reduce by 25%.

In separate pan, melt 25g *butter*, add 20g *flour*, slowly add 100ml *milk*. Add this slowly to chowder to thicken.

Add *clams & sweetcorn* – if raw, give 5 min; if cooked, just heat.

Top with diced *tomato* & chopped *chives*.

👤 Clam chowder is a must on the East Coast of America – a very special place for us. Sam was a 'West Wing' addict with a fascination for US politics & history. During Christmas 2007, he was very ill indeed in hospital. To cheer him up, I gifted him a trip to Boston, New York, Philadelphia, and Washington DC. As soon as he had recovered, we went there and had an incredible time. In 2016, we made the same trip with the 8yo, also exploring some of rural Virginia and Pennsylvania. This clam chowder is not 'authentic', but it's absolutely delicious, and connects me with very happy memories.

MACKEREL, RHUBARB and CUCUMBER

🐦 Mix 2 sliced *shallots*, 1tbsp *white wine vinegar*, 1tbsp *olive oil*, 2tsp *sugar*, *rhubarb* cut to 5 cm.

Roast, Fan 180, 10 min.

Lay *mackerel fillets* on top, roast 7 min.

Scatter *hazelnuts*, roast 5 min.

Serve with *crème fraiche*, sliced *cucumber* & *dill*, lots of *crusty bread*.

👤 On holiday in Padstow down in Cornwall, Sam loved to go out on the early morning mackerel boats and catch some fish for lunch. Me, not so much – sea-sicknesses tended to keep me shoreside! Once, when we were there as a family, I got an urgent phone call from the boat as he headed off down the estuary to tell me he'd 'accidentally' got on the wrong boat, and he wasn't just going to be gone for 2 hours but would actually be out for most of the day. I'm sure I detected glee in his voice at the thought of a relaxing child-free day doing one of the things he liked best. At least he brought back plenty of fish for tea!

This Scandinavian-inspired dish is light and refreshing – perfect for summer. If your rhubarb is tough, it may need to cook a bit longer.

SOLE MENUIERE with FRIES

SOLE MENUIERE with FRIES

Coat *sole fillets* in *seasoned flour*.

Fry in *butter & sunflower oil*, 2 min skin down, 1-2 min skin up. Rest.

Add 40g *butter* to pan, heat till brown & foaming.

Add *capers*, *chopped parsley* & a good squeeze of *lemon juice*.

Pour butter sauce over fish.

The 7yo loves fish and it is one of the simplest, fastest things you can cook. My fries have to be cooked in a proper deep fat fryer (see page 12) - I know it's probably not that healthy, but they just taste so much better than miserable oven chips. I remember in the early days of our relationship, one of the first things I bought for Sam when he moved into a new flat was a deep fat fryer. He thought I was mad - maybe I am - but a crisp bowl of salted rustling fries is total comfort food for me. Butter sauce and proper fries mean this dish isn't really in health food territory, but it's still lower in calories than a trip to the local chippy, and it tastes fab.

S&M² (SAKE, MISO, SOY, MIRIN) MACKEREL

🐦 Marinade *mackerel fillets* in 2tbsp *sake* (or *dry sherry*), 2tbsp *miso paste*, 2tbsp *mirin*, 1tbsp *soy sauce*, 1tbsp *caster sugar*, 1 crushed *garlic clove*, 10g *grated ginger* for 1 h.

Grill fish under medium heat until just cooked, ca. 5 min.

Sprinkle with *sesame seeds* (optional). Serve with *rice & pickles*

👤 The flavours of this dish take me back to Takayama, a rural Japanese town up in the mountains, famous for its sake, miso, and beautifully preserved old town. We had a wonderful time exploring the traditional wooden buildings that line the streets, sampling different products – the photo shows Sam at a Sake brewery. This dish is healthy, very tasty and uses the classic Japanese combination that I refer to as S&M² (yes, I know). It needs to be served with pickles – I like *quick pickled cucumber* (see page 160), but a jar of *Japanese pickles* from an Asian supermarket would be easy and more authentic. Finish with *leaves* (dress with *olive oil, sesame oil & rice vinegar*) or *edamame beans*, and boiled *Japanese rice* sprinkled with a little *Shichimi Togarashi*.

SALMON, FENNEL and DILL 'EN PAPILLOTE'

Par-boil *waxy potatoes*, 10 min. Cut in thick slices.

Melt 20g *butter*.

Place 1 portion sliced *potatoes*, sliced *fennel*, chopped *dill*, 10g melted *butter*, good squeeze *lemon* and 1tbsp *dry vermouth* (or *dry white wine*), on greaseproof paper. Top with 1 thick *salmon* fillet. Wrap. Repeat for portion 2.

Bake, Fan 180, 25 min.

The best salmon I ever ate was sitting at a restaurant on the dock in Seattle, watching the boats come and go across the Puget Sound. It was the last holiday Sam and I took together before we adopted our son, and we squeezed out every last moment of grown-up indulgence. We loved the Pacific Northwest – the amazing food & drink culture, the beautiful wild landscapes, and the laid-back liberal people. It's a stunning and welcoming part of the USA where we just felt instantly at home. This recipe is a *Diana Henry* invention from her fabulous cookbook *Simple*.

SEA BASS TRAYBAKE

Slice *potatoes*, add *olive oil*, season. Roast, Fan 180, 25 min.

Fry *mushrooms, garlic, thyme*. Add squeeze *lemon*.

Slash *sea bass* skin, stuff with *basil, parsley, thyme*.

Mix mushrooms with potatoes. Lay fish on. Roast, Fan 180, 10 min.

Serve with a sauce made with 2tbsp *olive oil*, 1tbsp *lemon juice, capers, parsley, basil*.

The 7yo and I got a rescue cat, Mittens (Mitts) – he is very patient, affectionate and is a massive fan of the days I cook fish. Sea bass is easy to cook and marries well with different flavours. This traybake, adapted from *Jamie Oliver*, served with 'Sauce Vierge', builds the dish on top of part-roasted sliced potatoes – if you want to make it fancier, use *wild mushrooms*.

This recipe is hugely adaptable – for example, change the mushroom mix for *red peppers, black olives & sliced lemon* to make the dish brighter and more spring/summer-like. Another good variation is *roast artichokes* from a jar with *herby/lemony marinated green olives*. The secret is to place the other ingredients into the roasting tray at the right time so that they will be cooked to your liking. As long as the fish gets 10 min on top at the end, and the potatoes have 30-40 min overall, you're winning. Essentially, it's a build it yourself ready meal.

MOROCCAN FISH and COUSCOUS

🐦 Mix 60g *flour*, 1tsp *paprika*, 1tsp *cumin*, ½tsp *cinnamon*, ½tsp *ground ginger*, 2 crushed *cloves*, *salt* & *pepper*.

Coat *haddock fillets* in spiced flour. Pan fry in *butter/oil*, 5-8 min.

Mix 100g *couscous*, 125ml *water*, 10g *butter*, *salt*, 5 min. Fluff up. Add chopped *dates*, *red pepper*, *parsley*, crushed *pistachios*.

👤 Underneath the aromatic, golden Moroccan-spiced crust is beautiful white flaking fish. It's paired with couscous which requires no more 'cooking' than pouring on hot water. It is important to load couscous with flavour & texture, or it can be dull. In this case, sweetness from dates (or *sultanas/dried apricots*), freshness from red pepper, herbal notes from parsley, and crunch from pistachios (or *toasted flaked almonds*). Serve with a wedge of *lemon*. If you want more heat, add ½tsp *cayenne pepper* to the spice mix, and scatter chopped *red chilli* over. You can replace the individual spices with ready-made *ras el hanout*. In Morocco, exploring Marrakesh's souk was a joy – every spice merchant makes their own unique *ras el hanout* mixed spice blend.

PAN-FRIED COD on CHORIZO & BEAN STEW

🐦 Prepare the stew as on page 11, replacing *chickpeas* with *cannellini beans*.

Season *cod fillets* (or other white fish) with *salt* and *pepper*.

Pan fry in *butter/olive oil* (1:1), medium heat, 5 min skin-side down, 1-3 min skin-side up. Adapt cooking time depending on thickness of fillet.

Serve fish on top of stew, scatter chopped *parsley* over.

👤 Based on the tweets I receive, *Chorizo & Chickpea Stew* is one of the most popular dishes in *tw-eat*. I put it at the front of the book because it represents my first date with Sam, but also because it really exemplifies the *tw-eat* approach of little effort and very simple instructions leading to deeply satisfying flavours. This recipe merely encourages you to pan-fry some white fish while the stew simmers – turning a simple midweek supper into a real luxury dish suitable for weekend indulgence or hassle-free entertaining.

SEARED TUNA 'NICOISE'

 Plate warm boiled *green beans*, chopped *tomatoes & cucumber*.

Dress: 2tbsp *olive oil*, 1tbsp *lemon juice*, chopped *basil*, 1tbsp *grain mustard*. Save some.

On very hot griddle, sear oiled *tuna steak* 1 min each side, turning through 90° after 30 s.

Dress again.

Serve with *fries* (unhealthy) or *crusty bread* (virtuous).

Sam loved tuna – ideally raw. This dish became a bit of a standard in our house, especially when we could sit out in the late afternoon sunshine in our little back yard. However, I would often annoy him by overcooking the tuna – so *really* don't hang about once it's in the pan. For the record, I know it's not really a niçoise – where are the *eggs, black olives,* and *red onions,* what is the mustard doing, and why is there cucumber in there? (Answer: the 7yo loves cucumber). Feel free to tweak the recipe to get it just how you want it, but the version here is how we like it!

HERB-ROLLED SALMON

 Cut *salmon* and roll in soft herbs (e.g. *dill, tarragon, parsley*).

Cut *courgette* into half-moons.

Cook *salmon & courgette* in pan with *butter* & a *little oil*, 5 min.

Add 2tbsp *creme fraiche & squeeze of lemon*.

Serve with fluffy, buttery *mashed potatoes*.

There's a time of year when we have a non-stop supply of courgettes coming from the allotment. This is probably my favourite way of using them up. The 7yo absolutely adores fish and mashed potato, so this ranks up there as one of his favourite dinners. Normally, I can't honestly be bothered making mash, but here, the fish is so simple that it's easy enough to get a good mash made on the side – as explained on page 16, I always use a potato ricer on boiled & dried potatoes for the smoothest mash possible, then add a generous amount of *butter, milk, salt,* and *pepper*.

SAM's MEXICAN FISH STEW

Sea bass, clams, prawns, tomato, onion, jersey royals, radish, sweetcorn, ancho chillies, deep-fried *tortilla, coriander.*

Sam was a brilliant cook – the photograph shows him as a teenager cooking for his family, something he always loved to do. This Mexican Fish Stew is something he made in 2018, the year before he died. It was both beautiful and delicious. I don't exactly know how he made it, and I can't find the recipe, so I have merely listed the ingredients – that was all I have on my original tweet. I can, of course, reconstruct a vague idea of how he did it. Shellfish cooked in a tomato-stew base, warmed with ancho chillies, the fresh vegetables dropped in late-on to keep some crunch. The deep-fried tortillas, a pan-fried fillet of sea bass and a scattering of coriander being added at the very end. I'm sure I could recreate something quite like it – but it wouldn't be exactly the same. It's worth sharing that this is actually the perfect analogy of how it feels when you are bereaved – a series of individual flavours of memories float around in your head, but you aren't always quite sure how to connect them into a coherent whole.

WHITBY CRAB CAKES (and SWEETCORN RELISH)

🐦 For 6 small crab cakes.

Take 1 *dressed crab*, gently mix with big handful *panko breadcrumbs*, ½ *beaten egg*, squeeze of *mayo*, squeeze of *lemon juice*, chopped *parsley*, *salt* & *pepper*.

Put in fridge to firm up a little. Shape into small patties.

Fry gently in *sunflower oil* and *butter*.

👤 The 7yo adores the seaside, and out on the East Coast of Yorkshire are some great places that we both love - Scarborough, Filey, Robin Hood's Bay. It's also the home of Whitby and its famous crab, some of the best in the UK. Sam adored crab and would always bring home a dressed crab whenever we went to the coast. It's a tradition I've continued, and crab cakes are something the 7yo and me both love to eat. Probably worth pointing out - that crab the 7yo caught is *not* a Whitby crab, it's just a little mud crab!

If you're interested, the sweetcorn relish in the photo is also cracking. (Sweetcorn Relish: fry 1 *shallot* till soft, add 2 cobs *fresh sweetcorn* kernels, chopped *red chilli*, 60ml *cider vinegar*, 25g *caster sugar* ½tsp *mustard powder*, boil 10 min).

PRAWN & COURGETTE TROFIE

 Cook 160g *pasta* (I used *trofie*).

Fine dice ½ large *courgette*, fry till golden in olive oil.

Add *prawns*, pinch *chilli flakes*, crushed *garlic* clove, 1 min.

Add 50ml dry *sherry/vermouth/white wine*. Reduce, 2 min.

Add chopped *basil*, juice of ½ *lemon* and cooked pasta.

This *Diana Henry* recipe is a delicious summer dish and a tasty way of starting to use up our annual courgette glut from the allotment. It's super quick to put together – in the way of many good pasta dishes, you can do all the prep for the sauce while the pasta is cooking, and then simply mix and serve. This is an ideal dish to enjoy sitting out in the garden with a nice crisp glass of white wine. Even if the weather is awful, and you are stuck in your kitchen for what seems like the 1000th day in a row in Covid lockdown, this will still somehow make you feel like you are on holiday.

ITALIAN SEA BREAM

 Fry sliced *spring onions, fennel, carrots* in *olive oil*, 4 min.

Add halved *cherry tomatoes*, 10 stoned *olives*, 2 cloves *garlic*, ½ *red chilli*, 2 min.

Score *sea bream*, stuff with *parsley & dill*, lay on top.

Add 150ml *white wine*, reduce by ½.

Add 300ml *water*, lid on, boil hard, 8min.

Serve with *lemon zest & herbs*.

A good recipe for whole fish is always useful. Sea bream cooked on the bone is, in my opinion, one of the most flavourful white fish you can eat, and this *Jamie Oliver* recipe is a cracker. Just serve it with good crusty bread.

I wasn't sure about feeding it to the 7yo, and carefully took his fish off the bone, leaving the head and skeleton on the side. Needless to say, that was *all* he wanted to look at - he was fascinated with the bones, the brain, and wanted to eat the eyes. Next time he'll just get the whole thing on the plate and can do his own fish surgery.

SEA BASS, OLIVES and FENNEL

🐦 Fry 1 sliced *red onion*, 1 clove *garlic, rosemary leaves*, pinch *dried red chilli*.

Add 120ml *white wine*, reduce.

Add chopped *fresh tomatoes, kalamata olives, capers*.

Separately fry sliced *fennel* till coloured.

Combine, roast, Fan 150, 30 min.

Fry *sea bass*, 4 min skin down, 1 min skin up, serve on veg.

👤 I've never been to the Greek islands, but this is how I imagine they taste. It is a part of the world I definitely want to discover with the 7yo. Travel is a massive part of my life – I love adventure, culture, and new experiences, sharing them with someone is really special. Planning new places to go is one of the things that helps keep me going through bereavement and single parenthood. I think the combination of Ancient Greek culture, sun-kissed beaches and fabulous food will make for two very happy travellers in the years to come.

BLOODY MARY PRAWN COCKTAIL

Chop ½ deseeded *cucumber*, small *avocado* & 1 *celery* stalk into dice. Add *cooked king prawns*.

Mix 150g *tomato passata* (or 150ml *tomato juice*), 1tbsp *Worcester sauce*, generous dash *tabasco*, good squeeze *lemon* juice, 1tbsp *vodka* (optional).

Mix all ingredients together and serve.

Sam loved a Bloody Mary – it was his brunch cocktail of choice on the morning after a 'long night'. One of my own guilty pleasures is a proper 1970s prawn cocktail. So, this Bloody Mary Prawn Cocktail recipe is the perfect marriage between us. We often had this as a starter on special occasions – it's great for perking up the palate before a blow-out meal. Obviously, you can adapt the Bloody Mary sauce to your own taste (and omit vodka for kids).

To make a classic prawn cocktail instead: use shredded *lettuce*, chopped *cucumber*, juicy *prawns*, *cocktail sauce* (make your own using 1:1 *ketchup:mayo* with a good dash of *Worcester Sauce*), *smoked paprika* and *lemon* wedges.

SMOKED HADDOCK with CHIVE SAUCE

 Place 2 *smoked haddock fillets* in frying pan, add 150ml *milk*.

Bring to boil, simmer uncovered 8-10 min. Remove fish.

Add 2-3tbsp *creme fraiche*, 15g *butter*, 1tbsp chopped *chives* & generous squeeze *lemon* juice. Heat until thickened, 2-3 min.

Serve with *mash & veg.*

This simple supper adapted from a classic *Delia Smith* recipe is very definitely the 8yo's 'happy place'. Ever since he was tiny, he has loved fish and cream sauce. It was something his foster mum used to cook for him before we adopted him, and I think that even still, it subconsciously makes him feel secure and contented.

If I'm being honest, I find making mashed potato a bit of a pain, but nothing else will do as an accompaniment here. The mash should be buttery, soft, and indulgent, almost melting into the creamy chive sauce. Using the poaching liquor as the base for the sauce gives it loads of flavour and means you don't need to add any salt (but do check by tasting). Amusingly, one of my Twitter friends pointed out that in this case, on the plate, I appear to have created the British Isles, with the sauce as the Irish Sea. It's a bit worrying that Scotland appears to be missing – I love it north of the border and after all, it's where the smoked haddock came from!

'BAKE-IN-THE-BAG' PRAWNS

Wrap in foil: 200g *raw prawns*, 1 quartered *cob sweetcorn*, 1 sliced *courgette*, 1 thin-sliced *lime*, chopped *coriander*, 2tsp *paprika*, ½tsp *cumin*, 1tbsp *olive oil*, 25g *butter*, *salt* & *pepper*.

Place foil on baking tray, Fan 180, 15-20 min until prawns are pink & veg tender.

'Cook' *rice noodles*, place in bowl, spoon contents of package over.

One of the easiest things you will ever make – and once you've got the hang of it, you can change things around very easily. Basically, in your package along with the prawns you need (i) vegetables that will steam nicely in ca. 15 minutes in the oven (most tender veg will be fine with this treatment), (ii) something acidic, (iii) flavourings/salt and (iv) oil/butter. Swap the *lime* for *lemon* or *rice vinegar* to send this in Mediterranean or Asian directions. Change the *Mexican spices* for *Mediterranean-style herbs* or *soy sauce & ginger*. Choose vegetables to your taste (*asparagus, green beans, mange tout, mini sweetcorn, peppers, spring onions*). Essentially, you are building a ready meal and then letting the oven and foil package do the work for you. Serve with *pasta, tortillas,* or *rice* instead of noodles.

GOAN FISH CURRY

 Heat 1tsp *coriander seed*, 1tsp *cumin seed*, 3 *cloves*, 4 *black peppercorns* in dry pan. Bash in mortar. Add 1tsp *chilli powder*, ½tsp *turmeric*.

Heat 2tbsp *sunflower oil* in frying pan, fry ½ chopped *onion*, 5 min.

Add 1tsp *mustard seed*, chopped *garlic* clove & 15g *ginger*, 2 min.

Add spice mix from mortar, 1 min.

Add 1 fine-chopped *tomato*, 1 whole *green chilli* (optional), ½tbsp *white wine vinegar*, 25ml *water*, 3 min

Add 100ml *coconut milk*, 100ml *water*, ½tsp *sugar*, ½tsp *salt*, 2 min.

Add *white fish* cut in cubes, 3-5 min till just cooked. Shake don't stir!

Add 1tsp *white wine vinegar*, season, add chopped *coriander*.

I was tempted to put this in the *Saturday Indulgence* section because it looks complicated – but it's not! If you have all the ingredients ready at the start, it only takes 20 minutes and delivers the tastiest fish curry. I made this for Sam sometimes when he came home from hospital. He wanted something light, but packed with flavour, the kind of thing that couldn't come off a trolley in an NHS ward. This hit the spot totally. Serve with *cardamon rice*.

FISH PIE JACKET

🐦 Bake, cut in half, & hollow out 2 *jacket potatoes* (save the potato!).

Gently fry 1 sliced *leek* in *butter*. Add to 150g mixed *fish*, 100g *creme fraiche, parsley, chives*, ½tsp *Dijon mustard, salt & pepper*. Put in jackets.

Mix potato, 50g *cheddar*, 1tbsp *creme fraiche*. Top jackets.

Bake stood in muffin tray, Fan 180, 25 min.

👤 Sam adored cooking a proper fish pie – it was one of his signature dishes – sadly I don't have his recipe any more. But in honesty, fish pie is a lot of effort to go to for supper, especially when it's just me and the 8yo. As soon as I saw this *John Whaite* recipe written down, I knew it was a winner. It gives you all the fish pie 'love' in a simplified easy-to-eat format. For ease, you can use frozen 'fish pie mix' (cod, smoked fish, salmon) from the supermarket – I also like to throw in a few shrimp or prawns from the freezer. We eat it sat in front of one of our favourite things on the TV, like Dr Who, holding the slightly cooled jacket and scooping out the hot fish pie filling with a fork. It's just a perfect recipe!

PRAWN & PEA RISOTTO

Finely chop and gently fry ½ *fennel* & ½ *onion* in *olive oil*. Do not colour. Add 1 sliced *garlic clove*.

Add 100ml *white wine*, reduce 50%.

Add 140g *Arborio risotto rice*.

Slowly add ca. 450ml hot *vegetable stock*, stir until rice is almost cooked.

Add 150g *raw prawns* & 2 handfuls *frozen peas*, stir until prawns are pink, ca. 3 min.

Add squeeze *lemon*, shredded *basil*, *salt* & *pepper*.

This is one of my most-cooked recipes over the years. It's adapted from a *Jamie Oliver* idea, but adding fennel into the base, because it is just such a perfect match with prawns and is a good way of getting an extra portion of hidden veg into the 8yo! Often risotto is a soothing, comforting dish, but this one is bright, fresh, and lively. It's one of the 8yo's favourite things to eat – clean bowl guaranteed every time.

SEA BASS on KOHLRABI with TARRAGON DRESSING

Peel, finely slice and quarter 1 *kohlrabi*. Add squeeze *lemon juice* & pinch *salt*. Leave 30 min, drain.

Mix small handful chopped *tarragon leaves*, ½ clove crushed *garlic*, ½tbsp *olive oil*, 40g *mayo* & squeeze *lemon juice*.

Mix kohlrabi & dressing. Add 25g toasted *pine nuts*.

Season *sea bass* fillets. Pan fry in *olive oil*, 3-4 min skin side down, ½ min skin side up.

Serve.

If you haven't tried kohlrabi this is one of the best introductions. It's crisp, cool, and juicy and sits just perfectly underneath a pan-fried fish fillet. It also works well in coleslaws as a replacement for cabbage (see page 145 for homemade coleslaw). And to get kids to give kohlrabi a go, what could be better than serving it with fish and chips? You know they won't go hungry, but they also get to add a new flavour to their palate.

CAJUN PRAWNS and RICE

Fry 1 clove chopped *garlic* in 1 tbsp *olive oil* & 10g *butter*, 2 min.

Add 200g *raw prawns* & 2tsp *Cajun spice*, 2 min.

Add 150g chopped fresh *tomatoes* & 8 thick-sliced *spring onions*, 3 min.

Add *cooked long grain rice* (from 150g dry rice), season if needed.

Finish with handful chopped *parsley*.

When we were a two-parent family, travel overseas to conferences and to meet collaborators was a key part of my job as a scientist. That has become much more challenging as a single dad. My final 'big solo trip' was to a conference in New Orleans – a city with an incredible food culture. This simple dish is inspired by my visit. For Cajun spices I use 'Joe's Stuff', which I bought while I was there. You can of course buy Cajun spice in a supermarket, or for fun make your own (blend: 3tsp *paprika*, 2tsp *garlic powder*, 2tsp *salt*, 1tsp *cayenne pepper*, 1tsp *onion powder*, 1tsp *black pepper*, 1tsp *onion powder*, 1tsp *dried oregano* & ½tsp *dried thyme*). Prawns are one of the 8yo's absolute favourite things to eat, so I often use them to introduce him to different flavours and tastes. It doesn't really matter what you do to them, he will still wolf them down, so it's a great trick for expanding his palate!

YUZU SCALLOPS, BACON CRUMB & MISO NOODLES

Marinade *scallops* in 1tbsp *soy sauce*, 1tbsp *mirin*, ½tbsp *yuzu juice*, 1tbsp *olive oil*, 5-10 min.

Grill 2 rashers *streaky bacon* to crisp - crumble.

Griddle *scallops*, 1-2 min per side.

Fry 3 sliced *spring onions*, 5g chopped *ginger* in a little *sesame oil*.

Add leftover marinade, 1tbsp *miso paste* & pre-cooked *udon noodles*, heat.

Serve with griddled scallops & crumbled bacon.

Yuzu is a great match for seafood, and when I found some fantastic scallops, I was inspired to create this dish. Scallops are a luxury ingredient – pairing them up with noodles is a good way to stretch them into a main course. We had this as part of a 'Japanese Day' where I introduced the 8yo to the culture of Japan. We made maki together (see page 216), learned how to write our names in Japanese calligraphy, wrote a haiku, watched a Studio Ghibli movie, and ate this for dinner – perfect!

MACKEREL TATSUTA AGE

Remove any bones from *mackerel fillets*, cut into bite-size pieces.

Marinade: 1tbsp *soy sauce*, 1tbsp *sake*, ½tbsp *mirin*, 5g grated *ginger*, 15 min.

Toss in *cornflour*.

Fry in hot oil, 170°C, 3-4 min.

Top with chopped *spring onion*.

Serve with a *soy sauce/mirin/rice vinegar* (1:1:1) dip, *jasmine rice*, *edamame beans* and a *lime wedge*.

Mackerel is a fish I associate strongly with Japan. One of my favourite food memories is of a fantastic lunch with Sam in Kyoto. The restaurant was tiny, with a beautiful little garden – the only thing on the menu was mackerel sashimi. The chef was so delighted to have English guests, that although he had very little English, he came to talk to us about his love of Manchester United and the fact that mackerel was his soul food – the one thing he was totally passionate about cooking. This *Harumi Kurihara* dish is deeply addictive mackerel soul food, and although a very different outcome for the fish, is dedicated to that memory. *Edamame beans* may seem exotic, but you can buy them frozen in the supermarket – just boil them (in their pods) like any frozen veg, sprinkle them with sea salt and serve.

MEDITERRANEAN MONKFISH TRAYBAKE

In roasting tin, drizzle *olive oil* on halved *cherry tomatoes*, sliced *red pepper*, ¼ chopped *red chilli*.

Roast, Fan 180, 8 min.

Roll *monkfish fillets* in *lemon zest*, chopped *rosemary* & *salt*.

Fry monkfish in *butter* till golden, spooning butter over, 3 min.

Add handful chopped *black olives*, *basil* & monkfish to roasting tin, Roast, 7 min.

Slice fish, serve with *parmentier potatoes*.

Monkfish is expensive, so this is a bit of a luxury supper, but it's so delicious – both fishy and meaty – and it stands up very well to strong Mediterranean flavours. Black olives (perhaps surprisingly) pair perfectly with fish and form the umami backbone of this dish. Parmentier potatoes are described earlier in the book, but for ease of reference: cube *potatoes*, *season*, toss in *olive oil*. Roast, Fan 180, 30-40 min. This makes effective use of the oven – just start the potatoes 20 minutes before the vegetables go in. Sometimes, I invent and cook a dish that I really wish Sam was still here to taste and enjoy – this was one of those occasions.

SIMPLE SUPPERS – VEG

ASPARAGUS & GOAT CHEESE TART

🐦 Blanch ca. 12 *asparagus* spears in boiling water, 1-2 min.

Mix 100g *soft goats cheese*, 50g *cream cheese*, 1tsp *thyme* leaves.

Cut *puff pastry sheet* to fit asparagus (with a border).

Spread cheese mix on pastry leaving border. Arrange asparagus on top.

Brush border with beaten *egg*.

Bake, Fan 180, 25-30 min.

👤 This is a perfect dish for kids to prepare, as most of the work is in the preparation of the tart – like baking but without an unhealthy sugar-filled product (much as I enjoy such things from time to time)! The 8yo loves making it, and as a massive fan of asparagus, he likes eating it too. It's a perfect Spring tart when asparagus is in season at the local shops. It is best served with a mixed dressed salad, ideally including some fragrant herbs. Obviously, the basic idea is versatile, for example, it would work very well with sliced *mixed peppers* (no need to blanch) instead of the asparagus.

VEGETABLE TEMPURA with SOY GINGER DIP

🐦 Dipping sauce: 2tbsp *soy sauce*, 2tbsp *mirin*, 2tbsp *rice vinegar*, 1tbsp *fish sauce* (optional), 5g grated ginger.

Batter: 60g *plain flour*, 60g *corn flour*, 150ml ice cold *fizzy water*. Mix very lightly with chopsticks – don't worry about a few lumps.

Dip *vegetables* (e.g. sliced *pepper*, sliced *mushrooms*, whole *asparagus*) in batter, deep fry in *oil* (180°C) until crisp & pale gold.

Drain on kitchen roll, serve immediately.

👤 One of the most evocative places I ever went with Sam was Mount Koya in Japan. It is the religious centre of the Shingon Buddhists, who adhere to a strict Shojin Ryori vegan diet. We stayed the night in a monastery, which was an incredible and tranquil experience. We were served a beautiful dinner, including the most perfect tofu, and show-stopping vegetable tempura. The following morning, we got up early for a Buddhist prayer service, then walked in the mist and fog through the atmospheric Okunoin cemetery to the Hall of Lanterns, where two lanterns, one donated by an Emperor, one by a peasant woman, have been kept burning continuously for almost 1000 years. The resonant living culture, food, and unique atmosphere will stay with me forever.

'SMOKY' AUTUMN PASTA

Crush 1 clove *garlic* and fry in generous *butter*.

Add 200g dry *pasta*, 500ml *veg stock*, 200ml *milk* and *thyme*.

Bring to boil, simmer 15 min until 'saucy', with pasta al dente.

Add 60g soft/melty *smoked cheese* and *black pepper*.

Heat through, serve with more *black pepper*.

This recipe is adapted from *Nigel Slater* and is the craziest way you will ever cook pasta! The pasta is cooked *in* the sauce, releasing its starch into what you eat – but it seriously works. I pair it with a crunchy pepper & cucumber salad with a sharp lemony salad dressing on the side for contrast. The flavour this delivers amazed me when I first cooked it. I was feeling really low at the time, missing adult dinnertime conversation and Sam's smiling face across the table. This dish was so comforting and warming, it was just like getting the big hug I was longing for and couldn't have.

SUMMER GNOCCHI SALAD

🐦 Boil *gnocchi*, 1-2 min.

Fry *gnocchi* in olive oil & butter until golden, then add chopped *garlic*.

Chop, slice, and mix fridge-cold *heritage tomatoes, radishes, spring onions* & *parsley*.

Mix and serve.

👤 The greengrocer on the local high street has the most amazing seasonal produce – they did me proud with the beautiful heritage tomatoes that are the making of this visually stunning *Nigel Slater* dish. This is a taste of summer on a plate, perfect for eating in the garden under the hot summer sun. It's a really interesting and unique way of presenting what is, essentially, a salad. I have to be honest; this dish was not the 7yo's favourite – he loves gnocchi, and they got demolished, but tomatoes and radishes are both towards the bottom of his list. Still, he was full, and I was happy.

HALLOUMI ROAST VEGETABLES

Roast mid-sized cubed *potato*, slightly larger cubed *sweet potato*, 2 bashed *garlic* cloves & *thyme* with *olive oil*, *salt* & *pepper*, Fan 180, 15 min.

Add *red onion* wedges, 15 min.

Add sliced *red & yellow peppers*, 15 min.

Add sliced *halloumi*, 10 min.

Serve

As ever in a traybake, the secret is making sure everything has just the right amount of time in the oven. It takes an hour all in, but it's hardly high-intensity cooking – you can easily get on with other jobs while it does its thing. This is a very tasty dish – when I have shared it on Twitter it is clear that many people already have their own variants of this excellent recipe. My original inspiration for this particular combination was *Nigella Lawson*, but all kinds of other veg roasted, and topped with halloumi would taste great.

CHEESE & ONION TART

 Gently fry 3-6 sliced *onions, thyme, salt, pepper* in 50g *butter* until soft.

Place *puff pastry* sheet on baking tray, add *onions* leaving 2cm border. Brush border with leftover onion butter.

Add 100g *gruyere*. Sprinkle 25g *parmesan* on top.

Bake, Fan 200, 20 min.

Serve with dressed *salad*.

Shamelessly adapted from my hero *Nigel Slater*, even down to the fact that because it's photographed with beer in his cookbook, it always makes me crave a glass (as you can see). The tart is quite rich, so make sure you dress the salad with a sharp acidic dressing – I use an *olive oil* and *balsamic vinegar* mix, with plenty of *black pepper*. The basic concept of an open tart on shop-bought puff pastry is super-versatile. Put whatever you want on top, and as long as it bakes nicely in 20 minutes, that's dinner sorted. You can do a nice light version with *tomatoes, mozzarella* and *basil* that sends the whole thing in a pizza-tart direction.

KALE & CANNELLINI BEAN PASTA STEW

 Fry chopped *bacon* (optional), then 1 chopped *onion* & *carrot*.

Add chopped *garlic* clove, 2tsp *tomato puree*, *thyme*.

Add *chicken stock* & *water* (750ml total). Boil.

Add can *cannellini beans* & 100g *pasta*, boil 5 min.

Add *kale*, simmer 7 min.

Season, stir in handful *parmesan*. Serve with *parmesan*.

A great one pot pasta soup/stew recipe that is both filling and satisfying, this was a massive hit with the 7yo. The broth is seasoned by the parmesan – if you want to give it even more savour, drop a parmesan rind in with the pasta and lift it out at the end. You can probably get away without crusty bread, as this is a very hearty soup, but you might want some to help mop up the juices.

CAULIFLOWER CHEESE PASTA

🐦 Fry florets from 1 small *cauliflower* in 25g *butter* & 1 tbsp *oil* till lightly golden.

Cook 200g *pasta*,

Add 150ml *double cream*, 100g *cheddar*, 50g *parmesan*, *black pepper*, heat.

Add pasta, top with *dill*, serve.

👤 Kids always love pasta, and the 7yo is no exception. This dish is a mash-up of cauliflower cheese and macaroni cheese and is a nice way of getting vegetables enthusiastically eaten. An alternative approach is just to mix leftover cauliflower cheese with pasta, but in this recipe, I think the crisp fried cauliflower against the soft pasta and creamy cheese sauce is just fab. You may wonder why the cauliflower is fried in both butter and oil – in fact this is something I do a lot throughout the book. The butter is for flavour and browning, the oil is there to stop the butter burning. This recipe is adapted from *Nigel Slater* and exemplifies everything that is good about his simple, yet clever, flavour-filled cooking style.

HALLOUMI FINGERS and AUBERGINE MASH

🐦 Roast halved *aubergine* & 2 whole *garlic* cloves in *olive oil*, Fan 180, 45 min.

Scoop *aubergine* flesh, mash with soft *garlic* innards, add 1tbsp *olive oil* & squeeze of *lemon*.

Cut *halloumi* fingers. Coat: *seasoned flour, egg, panko*. Fry till golden.

Scatter *pomegranate* seeds & *mint* leaves.

👤 Sam hated aubergines with a passion – he just wouldn't let me cook them, even though obviously, he never said this in front of the 7yo as it would have broken our 'family food rules'. Funnily enough, the 7yo also won't eat them. I hoped this *Nigel Slater* dish would convert him – it didn't, but I think it's delicious. Next time, I will keep the halloumi fingers but combine them with some mashed *beetroot* (roast *beetroot* in oil, then puree with a little *butter* and *crème fraiche*). On colour grounds I'd then have to drop the pomegranate – maybe throw in some toasted hazelnuts instead. Alternatively, I'll just serve the halloumi fingers with chips and beans.

MUSHROOM & SAGE GNOCCHI

 Fry 2 chopped *shallots* in *butter*.

Add 200g *mixed mushrooms*, fry, season, add 50ml *white wine* & a few chopped *sage* leaves.

Fry *gnocchi* in *butter* till golden (no need to boil them).

Add *mushrooms* to *gnocchi*. Top with crispy fried *sage*.

There's nothing hugely innovative about this classic combination of flavours, which is pure comfort food for a damp foggy evening. But frying the gnocchi just elevates them to pure indulgence – the crisp, golden exterior giving way to the soft, doughy, pillowy interior is perfection. Crispy sage leaves on the top finish it in style. This is the kind of supper the 7yo loves, and if he's been good, it's the kind of thing he gets to eat in front of his favourite Netflix cartoon.

CAVOLO NERO & HAZELNUT PAPPARDELLE

Cook ca. 200g *pappardelle*.

Cut 300g *cavolo nero* in ribbons and boil, 5 min, drain well.

Fry 1 chopped *garlic* clove in *olive oil*, add cooked cavolo nero.

Add cooked pasta.

Finish with handful *toasted hazelnuts*, chopped *flat leaf parsley*, 2tbsp *olive oil* & grated *pecorino*.

I grow cavolo nero on the allotment with the 8yo. In honesty, I think the slugs probably get as many leaves as we do, but we have great fun collecting a handful each time we go to the allotment during the Autumn and deciding what to do with them. This was one of our favourite outcomes. If your cavolo nero has tough 'ribs' in it, cut those out when you slice it. This is a version of a *Diana Henry* dish from her must-buy book *Simple*. She adds *red chilli* and a little *orange zest* with the garlic, so do feel free, but I found this version was more 8yo-friendly and tasted just as good. She also uses *parmesan*, but I like the sharp nuttiness of pecorino. It's easy to omit the cheese or replace it to make a vegan version of the dish. This is a great Autumn/Winter pasta recipe – it's the crunch of the hazelnuts and the rich bitterness of the cavolo nero that make it a bit special.

GREEN CHILLI & MANGO CHANA DHAL

Add 125g *yellow chana lentils*, 100g fresh *chopped tomatoes*, ¼tsp *turmeric* to pan. Add 500ml *water*. Boil, then simmer 30 min.

In 1tbsp *sunflower oil*, fry 1tsp *cumin seeds*, 1 chopped *green chilli*, 150g 1cm-diced *mango*, 3 min (until mango starts to soften).

Add cooked lentils, stir.

Add 1tsp *salt*, ½tsp *sugar*, squeeze *lemon juice*, chopped *coriander*.

We eat vegetarian food one or two days a week, and increasingly, I am trying to incorporate a vegan meal. I'm not an instinctive vegan cook, so I need to hunt round for inspiration. This recipe came from *Nisha Katona*'s beautiful book *The Spice Tree*, which although not vegan, has some great ideas. I have made this on summer evenings – usually after a long, hot, stressful day. The refreshing sweet-sour flavours revive me, and the fruity mango puts a smile on my face.

I have been to India with work a couple of times and find the vibrant cities fascinating. Dhal was a key part of one of my most unique food experiences, when I visited the spectacular Golden Temple in Amritsar. Part of Sikh culture is to feed people in their temples. Join the line, and you become one of the thousands of people every day fed a simple but tasty dhal, sitting on the floor in long rows. Once you're finished, you take your plate with you and help with the washing up. A memorable experience in a beautiful place.

CHIPOTLE HALLOUMI WRAP

 Cut 160g *halloumi* in 1-2cm cubes.

Fry halloumi in *sunflower oil* until golden with 1 rough chopped *yellow pepper*, ½ rough chopped *red onion* & 1tsp *chipotle chilli flakes*.

Make salsa (fine-chop *tomato, red onion, coriander, green chilli*, add good squeeze *lime* – see below for suggested amounts).

Place halloumi mix on warm *tortilla*, add salsa and *sour cream*.

So tasty – honestly, I struggled to photograph it before we ate it. Wraps are great family food. Everything sits in bowls on the table, and people just take as much of all the different things as they want. This is one of the 8yo's favourite ways of eating and avoids stress at the table. If you are cooking for chilli-sensitive kids, then leave the chilli flakes out of the halloumi/veg mix and dial down the chilli in the salsa. You can put a bottle of *chipotle hot sauce* on the table. Making a homemade fresh *pico de gallo salsa* is a useful skill – you can match the ratios of ingredients to your family's palate. As a starting point, for 2 people try: 2 *tomatoes*, ¼ *red onion*, ½ *green chilli*, handful *coriander*, good squeeze *lime*. I think it's better to very finely hand-chop everything with a good knife – if you use a food processor, it turns to mush and, in my opinion, loses its freshness and character.

MUSHROOM RISOTTO with PARMESAN CRISP

Fry finely-chopped small *onion* in *olive oil* & *butter* till soft.

Add 200g sliced *mushrooms*, fry.

Add 150g *Arborio risotto rice* & 50ml *white wine*, stir, reduce 50%.

Slowly add ca. 500ml *vegetable stock*, stirring.

For parmesan crisps, put small piles of grated *parmesan* on lined baking tray, Fan 180, 5-8 min.

Finish risotto with knob *butter*, handful grated *parmesan* & *black pepper*.

Risotto is just the most comforting thing to make and eat. The constant stirring is a kind of reflective kitchen therapy for the soul, and the soft textures and gentle autumnal flavours here are deeply soothing. If you want to tweak this recipe slightly, add some thick chopped *Italian salami* – it's great, but then it doesn't really fit in the vegetarian section. Parmesan crisps are not an essential addition, but they do make the risotto feel a little bit more special. The 8yo loves them and they effectively cook themselves while you do all that stirring and reflect on how your life could have been different.

BUTTER TOFU CURRY with SPINACH

 Fry 1 chopped *onion* in *butter* & *oil* until golden, 5-10 min.

Add 1tsp each *ground cumin*, *ground coriander*, *garam masala*, *turmeric*, 1 min

Add 2tsp *tomato puree*, 2 min.

Add 250g *passata* (or *chopped tomatoes*), simmer.

Rip 220g *firm pressed tofu* into chunks, toss in *cornflour*, fry in *sunflower oil*, until golden, drain.

To curry, add the fried tofu, 250g *spinach*, 100ml *coconut cream*, 10g *butter*.

Top with sliced *red chilli*.

This recipe is adapted from *Bosh*, the bestselling vegan cookbook – it's a simple mild 'butter chicken style' curry and has become a firm favourite of the 8yo. The recipe uses firm pressed tofu, which has a chewy, meaty texture. You can buy pressed tofu (here in the UK we love the Tofoo brand), but you can also take soft tofu and press it yourself between clean kitchen towels with something heavy on top (30 min+) to remove the moisture and firm it up. If you've never tried tofu before and are a bit sceptical about it, cook this recipe and you will definitely be converted!

COURGETTE & FETA FRITTERS

🐦 Grate 500g *courgettes*, sprinkle with *salt*, stand in sieve, 30 min. Gently squeeze, drain.

Mix with 3tbsp *flour*, 1 beaten *egg*, 100g crumbled *feta*, 3 fine-chopped *spring onions* & handful chopped *dill* (or *mint*).

Shape into 6 fritters.

Fry till golden in *oil/butter*. Turn once carefully – fragile.

👤 Without doubt, courgettes are one of the most depressing vegetables you can grow on an allotment. Delicious when small and sweet, turn your back on the plant for just a week or two, and suddenly they balloon into gigantic marrow-sized monstrosities. Not only that, but one plant can produce such prodigious quantities of courgette, that I sometimes think a few fields of them could solve world hunger. The real problem though, is that although you end up with enormous quantities, they are just not the most inspiring thing to eat. I'm therefore always on the look-out for good courgette recipes - this is adapted from a *Nigel Slater* recipe and is one of my favourites. These fritters are great with salad, crusty bread, and a good quality spiced chutney.

GLAZED BEETROOT & APPLE with CELERIAC MASH

Boil 2 *potatoes* cut in 3cm chunks, 5 min. Add ½ *celeriac* cut in 3cm chunks, 8-10 min.

Drain, dry, mash, dry, season, add 20g butter.

Melt 25g *light brown sugar*, add 25 ml *balsamic vinegar*.

Add 1 sliced *apple* & 3 roasted *beetroot* cut in wedges. Glaze, 3 min.

Finish with toasted *hazelnuts*.

The first time I took Sam out for dinner in York, way back in 2006, I knew that given his love of good food, it had to be somewhere special. One of the most unique places in York at the time was *Vanilla Black*, a tiny innovative restaurant cooking high-end vegetarian food. Sam was not initially impressed by the idea of a vegetarian restaurant, but we had a fabulous meal there, and in the process, I convinced him that I knew a thing or two about food! We were simultaneously disappointed and delighted when Vanilla Black closed in York but moved on to great acclaim in London. This dish is adapted from a recipe in the Vanilla Black cookbook. In honesty, it is somewhere between 'simple supper' and 'Saturday indulgence'. If you roast the beetroot yourself (peel 3 small *beetroot*, drizzle with *olive oil*, wrap in foil, roast, Fan 180, 50 min) it's weekend cooking, but if you use pre-cooked beetroot, it's a simple supper in 20 minutes.

CHEESE & ONION CAULIFLOWER

🐦 In roasting tin, put *cauliflower* cut into florets, *onion* cut in wedges, a sprig of *thyme*, 2tbsp *olive oil*, *salt* & *pepper*.

Roast, Fan 180, 25 min. Toss.

Add grated *gruyere* (be generous). Roast, Fan 180, 5-10 min.

Serve.

👤 Don't tell the 8yo – because it's a family rule that we never talk about food in a negative way – but I really don't like boiled cauliflower. The crumbly texture with a slightly slimy exterior just repels me. However, roasted, it is a completely different vegetable – the heat and dryness of the oven encourages it to take on a nutty flavour, and the texture improves dramatically. Combining roasted cauliflower with the sweetness of roasted onions in this cheat's version of cauliflower cheese makes for a ridiculously tasty and simple dish. This is a staple in our house. It's just perfect with leftover roast meat and becomes the star of the plate – an unusual situation in which the meat is actually just the side dish. However, it would also be great on its own, or with a green salad and is one of the simplest, tastiest vegetarian suppers you will ever make.

BAKED CAMEMBERT and CRANBERRY

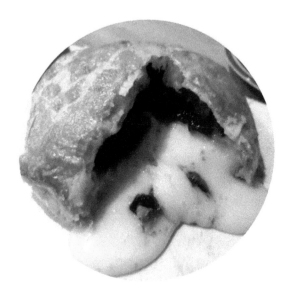

 Place a *puff pastry* sheet on a lined baking sheet.

Spread a circle with *cranberry sauce*.

Place a '*baking camembert*' on top. Fold pastry over and trim.

Flip it over so the folds are now on the bottom.

Egg wash, bake, Fan 190, 30 min.

Did someone say calories? This is just the best Christmas food you will ever eat – and it's so easy. Three shop-bought ingredients washed with egg and baked until the cheesy deliciousness oozes out all over your plate. Serve it with a salad dressed with a very sharp vinegary dressing. This is a dinner where afterwards I definitely plan to simply relax on the sofa with the 7yo, hopefully both snuggled up in front of a Christmas movie.

INDONESIAN TOFU & GREEN BEAN 'SATAY'

Chop *red onion*, 2 cloves *garlic*, 10g *ginger*, *red chilli*, fry in *oil*, 5 min.

Chop & add 4 *tomatoes*, 5 min.

Add 200ml *coconut milk*, 1tbsp *soy sauce*, 1tsp *brown sugar*, 10 min.

Add 150g halved *green beans*, 5 min.

Add 200g cubed *firm pressed tofu*, 5 min.

Stir in 1-2tsp *peanut butter*, top with crushed *peanuts*, serve with *rice*.

This is a very easy, fragrant curry – if you're a vegan-sceptic, I think this is the dish to convert you! The level of heat can be easily adapted by deciding how much red chilli to add – for a 'warming' child-friendly version of the dish, I just use half a red chilli. We had this sat in front of the TV watching Star Wars and the 8yo demolished it! He even tore himself away from the on-screen action to head off to the kitchen to get the pan and hunt for any leftover bits of tofu!

BEETROOT & ONION DHAL

Finely-dice & fry 1 *onion*, 1 clove *garlic*, 10g *ginger* in *oil*.

Add 2tsp *Madras curry* powder, 150g *red lentils*.

Add 200ml *coconut milk*, 200ml *water*. Simmer 15 min.

Fry 1 sliced *onion* until brown, add 1 tsp *yellow mustard seeds*, ½ tsp *chilli flakes*.

Briefly stir *cooked beetroot* through dhal, top with *natural yoghurt* & fried onions.

This delicious idea is borrowed from *Nigel Slater*, but I have swapped-out his simpler dhal recipe for my own slightly more complex, but favourite dhal (the first 3 lines of the recipe give you the basic dhal). The dhal recipe here is amazing just on its own with rice or flatbreads, but with the additions of beetroot, yoghurt and onion suggested by Nigel, it is taken over the top to a magical place. It's a wonderful soothing plate of gently spiced comfort food. Make sure you only very briefly stir the beetroot through the dhal at the end, or the whole dish goes pink! The 7yo absolutely adored this – beetroot is his favourite vegetable.

BROAD BEAN & GOAT CHEESE RISOTTO

Pod *broad beans*, boil 3 min, remove shells.

Fry ½ chopped *onion* in *olive oil*, add 1tsp *thyme* leaves.

Add 150g *Arborio rice*, 50ml *white wine*, reduce.

Slowly add 500ml hot *veg stock*, stir.

Add 50g *soft goat cheese*, pre-cooked *broad beans*, *black pepper*.

Dot with extra *goat cheese* & drizzle *olive oil*.

We grow broad beans on the allotment and in their short season, I love to cook with them. This simple risotto is a perfect vegetarian spring dish, with the sharpness of the goat's cheese lifting the rich savoury risotto. The 8yo adores rice, and it doesn't matter what I put in a risotto, it always gets wolfed down, so it's also perfect family cooking from my perspective!

When cooking with broad beans, unless they are *very* young and tiny, I prefer to remove both the pod *and* the outer shell from the bean. This is simple to do – after podding the beans and briefly boiling them, you then allow them to cool and simply squeeze the bottom of the shell – the intense green heart of the bean then just pops out.

CRUNCHY PANEER & SPINACH CURRY

 Chop & fry 2 small *onions*. After 5 min, add 2 chopped cloves *garlic* & 15g grated *ginger*. Continue until onions are golden.

Add 1tsp *ground cumin*, 1tsp *ground coriander*, 1tsp *turmeric*, 1tsp *salt*, 1 min.

Add 400g *can tomatoes* & 1 whole *green chilli*, 20-30 min.

Cut ca. 200g *paneer* into cubes, toss in 3tbsp *semolina* & 1tsp *garam masala*. Fry in *sunflower oil* until golden, 5 min.

Add 250g *baby spinach* to curry, 2 min.

Add crunchy paneer, squeeze of *lemon* juice, *black pepper*. Serve.

This is a fantastic, simple, curry and was one of Sam's favourite dishes to eat and cook. I love paneer curries too and always choose to eat them when visiting India. The crunchy coating for the paneer here is a clever *Hairy Bikers* idea, and adds texture to the dish, something that's sometimes missing in vegetarian food. This curry is guaranteed to convert the most reluctant carnivore to vegetarian food and is perfect with naans or flatbreads.

SPAGHETTI 'RIANIMARE'

🐦 Cook 150g *spaghetti* in salted water.

Chop large handful *black olives*, the rind of ½ small *preserved lemon*, ½ *red chilli*, handful *parsley*.

Stir chopped ingredients into cooked pasta with a good glug *olive oil*.

👤 Christmas 2020! On December 23rd, my 'Covid tracker app' sent me a notification to say we had to isolate until the New Year. Our modest Christmas plans got written off and the 8yo and me hunkered down in the kitchen. At least the shopping was done, and we had lots to sustain us. Once self-isolation was complete, the 8yo went off to spend a day with his Nanny & Grandad - our support bubble. As I collapsed at my kitchen table and looked at the bombsite of a house after 8 days of enforced Christmas house arrest, I just wanted to eat something reviving after all the excess of Christmas food. This bowl of pasta completely hit the mark. It combines salty, sour, hot, and fragrant, with these four key components delivering a big flavour punch. Even better, this requires no cooking other than boiling a pan of spaghetti. In the recipe, I suggest 75g pasta per person, a good size for a light lunch - use 100g each for a dinner sized portion, but it's not really a dinner pasta. I have called it spaghetti 'rianimare' - before the purists complain, this is not a 'real' Italian dish, but I did feel truly 'revived', so I think the name is wholly appropriate.

POP's PASTA

Sweat two thinly sliced *red onions* in *olive oil* until soft.

Add ½tsp *marmite*, ½tsp *flour*, pinch of *salt*.

Add 100ml *water*.

Very gently heat, 30 min, replenish water if needed.

Cook 200g *pasta*, add to sauce.

Finish with a knob of *butter*, grated *parmesan* & *black pepper*.

Marmite was one of Sam's favourite foods. As he became very ill towards the end, one of the few things he wanted to eat was Marmite on Toast. In fact, the tradition became so established, that we even have an empty jar of Marmite in our memory box. The 7yo likes to take the lid off and sniff it when he is looking through Pop's old things and remembering. This simple supper is therefore a memory box meal, and a big warm umami hug from Pop, in a bowl – that's why in this house, we call it 'Pop's Pasta'.

'Marmite pasta' was popularised by *Nigella Lawson*, but this is actually an adaptation of a recipe from *Anna del Conte* (Italy's version of *Delia Smith*). Using this much marmite only really adds savour to the dish – if you want it more 'marmitey', just add a bit more.

A QUICK TEA

CRAB & PEA PASTA

🐦 Cook 175g *pasta* (I used *trofie*)

Fry 1 sliced *garlic* clove in 25g *butter* until soft.

Add 150g *crab meat*, 150g *frozen peas* & a good squeeze of *lemon*. Heat until peas are defrosted.

Add 2tbsp *double cream*, season with *salt* & generous *black pepper*, stir through cooked pasta.

👤 The Yorkshire Coast is one of the 8yo's favourite places – he once told me: "Daddy, it makes me happy in my heart when we go to the beach". As soon as we get to the beach, he pulls off his shoes and socks, and just runs for the sea with a massive grin on his face. It's a shame we don't live closer to Cornwall – I'm sure he'd grow up to be a surfer dude! I sometimes cook this pasta dish if we bring home a dressed crab. More often, however, I use one of the pots of crabmeat you can buy in most supermarkets. Like all the best pasta dishes, it is very simple and only takes as long to put together as the pasta takes to cook. As the 8yo gets a little bit older, this is exactly the kind of thing I could imagine him cooking by himself, especially if he is feeling a bit sad, and wants to use a simple supermarket ingredient to transport him to his happy place at the seaside.

CRUMPET RAREBIT

🐦 Gently soften ½ sliced *leek* in butter, 5-10 min. Do not colour.

Add 2tsp *flour*, 150ml *double cream*, 75g grated good *red cheese*, 1tsp *Dijon mustard.*

Grill 3-4 *crumpets* on bottom side.

Top with cheesy mix. Grill until golden.

👤 OK, so it's not really a rarebit, but the use of leeks is kind-of Welsh. Putting it on a crumpet makes for the perfect hand-held cheesy, creamy, oozy snack. It really does need a crunchy salad on the side to help cut through the richness though. This adapted *Nigel Slater* recipe can itself, easily be adapted further – replace the leeks with onions for a cheese and onion version. More radically, replace the red cheese with a soft *blue cheese* and the leek with *apple*. Or just go 'full rarebit', get rid of the cream, replacing it with a little less *beer* and a splash of *Worcester sauce*. Basically, it's easy, it's cheesy, and more importantly, when you feed it to the 8yo, he happily sits on the sofa and eats it while watching Netflix. Simple teas like that are worth their weight in gold.

FISH FINGER TACOS

Cook 6-8 *fish fingers* according to pack instructions. Cut into 4.

Mix 1 chopped *avocado*, 3 chopped small *vine tomatoes*, ¼ fine-chopped *red onion*, ½ chopped *jalapeno chilli*, small handful chopped *coriander*, juice of ½ *lime*.

Mix 3tbsp *sour cream*, 1tbsp *mayo*, 1tbsp *sriracha*, juice of ½ *lime*.

Serve on warm *tortillas*.

I guarantee that kids will love these fish finger wraps, and it mixes things up a bit from the usual fish fingers, chips & beans. You can tailor the chilli content to taste – it's easy to hold back on the chillies and then add extra chillies to a separate adult portion. This is one of those meals where we put bowls on the table and help ourselves to whatever we want – interactive eating. To make the wraps close to being proper tacos, buy mini wraps, or cut larger wraps into smaller circles. They become proper hand-held morsels – the 8yo always manages to surprise me with just how many he can eat! This is a perfect tea for the end of the week – other than chopping, mixing, and putting some fish fingers in the oven, it's no effort for loads of flavour and lots of fun.

SPAGHETTI CARBONARA

 Cook 200g *spaghetti*.

Fry chopped *bacon* in *olive oil*. Add diced *shallot* and merest ½ clove *garlic*. Set aside.

Mix 1 *egg*, grated *parmesan*, *black pepper* and 25ml *double cream*.

Drain spaghetti into large bowl, add egg mix & bacon mix. Stir.

Serve with *parmesan* & generous *black pepper*.

An absolute family favourite, spaghetti carbonara is a mainstay of our kitchen appearing on the menu probably once a month. It's fast, being cooked from start to finish in 15 minutes, and it's tasty. On Twitter, I have had much 'discussion' with Italian friends about my recipe – I *know* it's not authentic – Italians do *not* add cream. But I like a splash, because it makes the sauce silkier, and helps stop the egg scrambling in the hot pasta. I also add a splash of milk to my scrambled eggs and omelettes, so there! If you don't like the addition of cream, just leave it out, and perhaps add an extra egg. Italians also do not use garlic, but again, just the slightest whiff of it really enhances this dish for me. It's a rich dish, so I use plenty of black pepper.

SWEETCORN POPPERS

 Mix 3 cobs of *fresh sweetcorn* kernels, 75g shredded *mozzarella*, 75g *cream cheese*, 2 chopped *spring onions*, ¼tsp *chilli powder* (opt.).

Add 40g *cornmeal*, 30g *flour*, 1 *egg*.

Shape as balls, coat in mix of 75g *panko breadcrumbs* and 25g grated *parmesan*.

Fry in hot *oil* until golden, 6 min.

Who said vegetarian food can't be a little bit indulgent and even 'dirty'? These poppers are perhaps the best way I have discovered of using up our sweetcorn glut from the allotment and make a simple, and very popular tea for the 7yo. You can deep fry the poppers, or just fry them in a wok with about 1" of sunflower oil. They need to be served with a dressed crunchy salad and some sort of sauce – the one here was a chipotle barbecue relish (out of a jar). This kind of tea is the perfect excuse for buying jars of relish at food festivals. Sam and I always loved going to the food festival in Wetherby with his family, tasting as much as possible and choosing the best produce. Pick your relishes well and they become 'hero ingredients', lifting up your simple tea and making it a little bit special.

LEFTOVER CHICKEN 'ALFREDO'

 Cook 200g *pasta*.

Finely dice ½ *fennel* & 1 *garlic* clove, gently fry.

Add *leftover roast chicken*, heat.

Add 100g grated *cheddar* & 100ml *creme fraiche*.

Use a little *water* to make sauce desired consistency. Season.

Add cooked pasta, serve.

When you're roasting a chicken for two, there are always leftovers, and they are some of my favourite things to cook with. This is a simple pasta dish perfect for the 7yo to eat in front of cartoons after a hard day at school. On this occasion I used pasta spirals, but I'm not sure they were best suited to the sauce – conchiglie or tagliatelle would probably be better. And a special message to Carmen, my incredible Italian post-doctoral co-worker, I know putting chicken in sauces is not very Italian and is, in fact, a New York American thing to do! I also know this is a massively shortcut 'Pasta Alfredo' and the use of fennel is a bit weird – that's fine by me, because it tastes great (and surely it's better than the alternative, which is opening a can of Heinz spaghetti hoops)?!

FILLY's BREAD & BUTTER LORRAINE 'EN MUG'

🐦 Melt a knob of *butter* in a mug in microwave.

Tear up 1 slice *white bread* very small. Add 1 beaten *egg*, 60mL *milk*, chopped *ham* (or *cooked bacon*), handful grated *cheddar*, *salt & pepper*.

Add to mug, microwave 1.5 min.

Turn out and top with grated *cheddar* while hot.

👤 One of the brilliant things about Twitter is the random connections you make, and the way in which they can enrich your life. Felicity (Filly) is a disability rights activist, who once studied Chemistry at The Open University. She shared this recipe with me, and I thought it was a fantastic thing to feed the 7yo for tea when I was pressed for time. How often do you find a recipe you can cook in a mug in less than 2 minutes, and that a hungry boy will devour and ask if there's another one?

CABBAGE and BACON PASTA

 Fry chopped *smoked streaky bacon.*

Add sliced *cabbage, thyme* a knob of *butter*, 1tbsp *water* & salt.

Heat with lid on until cabbage is soft.

Add cooked *pasta* & cubes of *mozzarella cheese.*

Stir and let cheese start to melt in residual heat.

Drizzle with *olive oil*. Serve.

This combination of cabbage and bacon is great – flavours we love in this house. It takes 15 minutes from start to finish and is perfect to put down in front of the 7yo for tea. I think I adapted the original idea from *Jamie Oliver*. I suspect it may be even better with *Taleggio* cheese stirred through in terms of flavour, but there is something about the cool milkiness of mozzarella just starting to melt that I adore in the mouth against the crispy bacon bits and the bite of the pasta.

FRENCH DIP

Oven-cook (or warm through) a *crusty baguette*.

Spread with *horseradish* and load with leftover cold *rare roast beef*.

Serve with *hot gravy*, *Dijon mustard* and *fries*.

OK, so it's 'just' a roast beef sandwich, but with a pot of hot gravy to dip it into, mustard *and* horseradish, and crisp, rustling fries on the side, it's a thing of total beauty. This sandwich was one of Sam's favourite things to eat when we were travelling in the USA. For the baguette, I use one of those part-cooked, bake-in-the-oven ones from the supermarket – in fact these very often fill the role of 'crusty bread' in our house. Purists will tell you the quality of gravy is key, and of course, you could save some of your beautiful handmade roast beef gravy (see page 168) to reheat. But I've made it with *Bisto*, and it still put a big fat grin on my face.

EGG IN THE HOLE

 Cut hole in a slice of *white bread* with a cookie cutter.

Heat *sunflower oil* in frying pan.

Add *bread* (and 'hole') and start frying.

After almost finishing one side, flip *bread* and add *egg* to hole.

Cook until bottom of *egg* is set & bread golden.

Flip back briefly (or put lid on pan) to seal top of *egg*.

Sam taught me this recipe – I'd honestly never seen it before. It probably takes the highest level of cooking skill of everything in this book! To get the egg, the bread, and the 'hole' all perfectly cooked requires exceptional feel, timing, and care – you want the egg to be mostly set, but just a tiny bit running in the middle, and the bread to be crisp and golden. You get the idea from the recipe – probably even just from the picture – find your own way of doing it to get it just right. The 7yo thinks it's a fantastic tea (when I get it right). He always says the hole is the best bit!

PAD THAI

 To a hot pan, add (in order):

Prawns. Spring onions. Egg.

Then 1 tbsp *fish sauce*, 1-2tbsp *sweet chilli sauce*, very good squeeze *lime juice*.

Add softened ('cooked') *rice noodles*.

Finish with crushed *dry roast peanuts*, *coriander* and lots of *red chilli* (for me).

Prawns are one of the 7yo's favourites, and this Pad Thai is so fast and tasty. It takes longer to get all the ingredients out of the cupboard than it does to cook it. This was always one of Sam's favourite teas as well, and making it is a bit of a ritual. It's become one of those dishes I can just cook without ever really thinking – that kind of cooking is very therapeutic. You can also add some halved *mange tout* along with the spring onions if you want more veg in the dish. A good friend of mine on Twitter told me this recipe had become a firm favourite of her kids, and was usually cooked by her husband. They called it 'Dad Thai' – I think that's just perfect!

PASSION FRUIT MERINGUE

 Whip *double cream* until it is just beginning to stiffen.

Place on a *meringue nest* – the very best you can buy.

Top with *passion fruit* pulp.

This is not a recipe, and I know *everyone* does this. It's just a reminder, mostly to myself, that it is possible to get a 'sophisticated' pudding down on the table in less than 5 minutes. Obviously, you can use other fruit on the top – *raspberries* are classic – but somehow, the ability of passion fruit to provide both flavour and a kind of sauce makes it ideally suited to the job. The secret here is to buy the very best meringue nest you can find. It absolutely must *not* be one of those bright white ones that shatters into dust like Plaster of Paris, rather one of the slightly dusky, pinkish-brown ones, that yields a fudgy interior. Yes, they cost more, but you are getting pudding in 5 minutes here. If you want to make the meringue nests yourself, just look it up on Google – honestly, this is not really the section of the cookbook for you!

GRILLED CHEESE and 'STUFF'

 *Butter* two slices *white bread.*

Make an 'inside-out' sandwich with filling (*grated cheese + stuff*) on the unbuttered side and buttered side facing outwards.

In dry frying pan, fry sandwich (ca. 2-3 min per side) until golden, press occasionally with fish slice.

If you do this already, you will think: "Why on earth did he put this in a cookbook? I want my money back!" But if you don't already do this, it will change your life! Sam introduced me to this super-quick lunch/tea and it's now something that I probably eat more than anything else. A bit like cheese on toast, but no need to get down on your knees and peer under the grill to see if it's done, and a meltier, softer easy-to-eat finish. A toastie without the mess of the toasted sandwich maker. It's endlessly versatile. Simple fillings would be *just cheese, cheese & ham, cheese & pickle, cheese & chutney,* even *cheese & tuna mayo,* but really your imagination can take you wherever you want. Got leftover *pico de gallo salsa* from Mexican night, put it with *cheese* for a spicy sandwich. Take fried *onions, mango chutney,* chopped *red chillies, coriander,* a pinch of *garam masala & cheese,* and you get a heavenly Indian-style sandwich. Grilled perfection.

BUBBLE & SQUEAK

🐦 Chop/mash leftover *roast potatoes, parsnips & veg.* (Add a little extra *mashed potato* – only if needed)

Mix in just enough beaten *egg* to bind. Season with *salt* & *pepper*.

Fry in a disc 1-2cm deep until golden, ca. 5 min, flip halfway.

Serve with leftover *roast meat* & *sauce.*

👤 Roast dinner leftovers are a great way of getting a quick Monday night tea on the table after that difficult first day of the week at work. The 8yo loves Bubble & Squeak, and often asks for it on Mondays – so it's not even like leftovers are unwelcome! Bubble & Squeak is a British classic, but often badly made, with mountains of mashed potato blanketing all the flavour. You *can* bulk this version out with extra mash, but it's better not to have to bother making mash – it also tastes better without. If you know you want Bubble & Squeak, cater Sunday lunch generously. Using leftover roast potatoes & parsnips gives depth of flavour. The leftover Sunday lunch veg are also added (throw in *frozen peas* if you are short). Bubble & Squeak is particularly good with pork & apple sauce, duck & cherry sauce, or beef & horseradish sauce – again, all leftovers. For more in-depth information on Sunday Roast cooking see the dedicated chapter.

ROASTED PEPPERS & BURRATA

Slice 2 *red peppers*.

Roast in *olive oil* with 1 crushed clove *garlic*, 1tsp *thyme leaves*, *salt & pepper*, Fan 180, 15 min.

Add 8 halved *cherry tomatoes* & ½ sliced *red chilli*, 15 min.

Serve with *burrata* & lots of *crusty bread*.

A delicious, simple, light tea, with fabulous colour and contrasting flavours and textures, that will make you feel like you're on holiday even if you're stuck in your own kitchen for the hundredth day of a Covid lockdown. If you want to smarten it up a bit and avoid the pepper skins, then first cut the peppers in half, grill them to blacken the skins, allow to cool, peel off the skins, and then slice the peppers. You can then mix the sliced peppers with all the other ingredients in the roasting tin and simply roast for 15 minutes.

This dish sparked a good discussion with the 8yo, which illustrates perfectly how we think and talk about food. He wasn't completely sure about the wet texture of the burrata, although he tried it and said it was 'ok'. He told me he would prefer the slightly firmer texture of *mozzarella* (which would also be fantastic in this dish – so it's a good call and illustrates that he has a great palate). Anyway, now I know, I can save some money on his portion and keep all the delicious, cool, milky, oozing, expensive burrata for myself.

OGGY's POT NOODLE HACK

Take lid off *Pot Noodle*, add *boiling water* to mark.

Also pour boiling water over small *frozen veg* (e.g. *peas, sweetcorn, chopped mixed veg*).

After 4 min, drain veg using sieve, add to Pot Noodle, stir, add sauce.

Deep breath – it's confession time! Sometimes, when I'm in a hurry, I give the 8yo a Pot Noodle. In Japan, where Instant Noodles are an acceptable part of life, this behaviour would be viewed as normal. However, in the UK, this is considered by some as the very worst in parenting, bordering on abuse. Certainly, when I shared this fact on Twitter, it evoked a strong response as you can see – although strong responses can, of course, be par for the course on Twitter. In some ways I agree, I don't really *want* to feed the 8yo Pot Noodles, but sometimes, needs must. Anyway, to save my blushes, Mark Ogden, a friend who many years ago I worked alongside in the lab in Oxford, shared this brilliant hack with me – Pot Noodle with extra veggies, so you can feed your kids in 4 minutes and feel less guilty. What did the 8yo think? 'Mmmmm, thank you Daddy, that was actual tasty'.

Replying to @professor_dave
There are so many more healthy and nutritional things one can prep in 10mins. Wonderful example of today's lamentable parenting.
9:53 · 23 Jan 20 · Twitter for iPhone

BACON-WRAPPED HALLOUMI

 Cut 160g *halloumi* into 'fingers', wrap each finger in a rasher of *streaky bacon*.

Fry in *sunflower oil* until golden.

Pour boiling water onto 200g *frozen peas*, drain. Add to 50g *watercress* and 4 sliced *spring onions*.

Dress greens: 1tbsp *olive oil*, 1tbsp *cider vinegar*, ½tsp *grain mustard*.

When I mentioned on Twitter that I had published *tw-eat*, this was the first dish one of my friends wanted to read in the book. Having forgotten to put it in first time round, and with it being one of my best family dishes, I knew that by popular demand, it simply had to appear in *tw-eat more*. The fresh sweet peas and bitter watercress are a delicious combination that both kids and adults will enjoy. If your kids really won't eat the watercress, does it matter? Just let them leave it. You can always replace watercress with some milder leaves like *lamb's lettuce* – but I do think the pepperiness of watercress is an integral part of the dish against the saltiness of halloumi and bacon.

1-2-3 PANCAKES

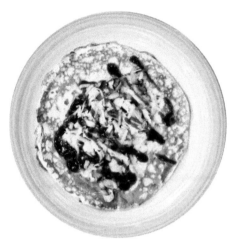

🐦 Put 100g *flour* in bowl. Add 2 *eggs*. Mix. Slowly add 300ml *milk*, whisking. Add pinch *salt*. Leave 30 min. (Makes 8)

Get *sunflower oil* very hot in frying pan – ladle in thin layer of batter, tilt pan to spread. Leave 1 min till golden. Shake to loosen. Toss.

Serve topped with whatever you want or keep warm in low oven.

👤 In this house, pancakes usually only happen on Shrove Tuesday. Every year, I think how tasty and easy they are, then forget all about them again. By putting them in the book, I will hopefully remember to cook them more often. The method is as easy as 1-2-3 (flour, eggs, milk). For toppings, I like leftover *roast chicken, mushrooms, spring onions, cheese & BBQ sauce,* but *cheese & fried mushrooms* are great. Or why not go crazy with leftover *lamb & mint sauce* or reheated *curry?* On Shrove Tuesday, sweet pancakes with *lemon & sugar* are practically the law. The recipe makes 8 full-size pancakes. In one way, it feeds 4. But if you want savoury & sweet pancakes, it feeds 2. If your child is the 8yo, it feeds him. If you want the respect of your kids, you must toss pancakes properly, by flipping in the air. As you can see, it's never too soon to practice (even if it is with a cold pan)!

OMELETTE

🐦 Beat 2 *eggs* with *salt & pepper* (and ca. 25ml *milk*, optional).

Get *butter* hot in frying pan – pour in egg, pull back edges of omelette as they set, tilt pan allowing liquid to run into gap.

Add toppings – e.g. grated *cheese*, fried *mushrooms* etc.

Heat, gently loosen from pan (use spatula if needed), cook until golden

Slide out of pan, allow to fall onto plate folded in half.

Serve with crunchy *salad, bread & butter*.

👤 I know that an omelette recipe is superfluous for anyone who has ever been in a kitchen, but the emotional significance of this dish is such that it really should be in the book. This is what I eat, sat on the sofa wrapped in a blanket, if I have been poorly. The pure comfort of egg and cheese is what I crave. Omelette (and scrambled eggs) have played this role for me ever since I was little. I stretch my eggs for both dishes with a little milk – probably because that's what my Mum always did – but it does also make the final texture softer and more soothing. The act of love in trying to produce a golden omelette that turns out of the pan perfectly for the 8yo when he has also been feeling poorly says more than any number of words can.

SATURDAY INDULGENCES

P&P PANCAKES, BACON and MAPLE SYRUP

🐦 Dry: 125g *plain flour*, 1tbsp *sugar*, 1tsp *baking powder*, ½tsp *salt*.

Wet: 120g *milk*, 1 *beaten egg*, 25g *melted butter*.

Mix wet into dry, throw in *blueberries* (optional).

Fry in the melted butter pan with *sunflower oil*. Flip when 'holes' appear & bottom golden.

Serve with grilled *streaky bacon* & *maple syrup*.

👤 Every Saturday, we'd always go to The Pig & Pastry for breakfast, before shopping on the local high street – the 'Bishy Road'. We were such regulars that Sam and I even appeared in their cookbook, back in our child-free days when we could relax at the counter with coffee and the papers. The 7yo loves their waffles & bacon. When lockdown came, I wanted to make Saturday mornings at home special. I couldn't master waffles, but I could cook pancakes. Although they have never appeared on the P&P menu, it is what I now cook in homage to them. The bacon must be streaky – the crispness when grilled is perfect. These pancakes are also brilliant served with fruit (*raspberries* or *watermelon*), and *black pudding* makes a great addition to bacon. The quantities will make two frying pans worth of pancakes – 2-3 servings.

APPLE & CINNAMON PANCAKES with ICE BERRIES

Dry: 125g *plain flour*, 1tbsp *sugar*, 1tsp *baking powder*, ½tsp *salt*, ½tsp *ground cinnamon*.

Wet: 115g *milk*, 1 beaten *egg*, 25g melted *butter*.

Mix wet into dry, add 1-2 peeled, cored, grated *eating apples*.

Fry in melted butter pan with *sunflower oil*. Flip when 'holes' appear & bottom golden.

Serve with handful of half-defrosted *berries* & *maple syrup*.

We have a lot of love for Saturday morning blueberry pancakes and bacon in this house (see the previous page). This apple & cinnamon version is a delicious way of re-inventing that recipe. The pancakes are great with bacon, or with raspberries or blackberries, but I think they are particularly good with 'ice berries'. What do I mean? Basically, I mean you get some berries out of the freezer, and then because it's early in the morning, you don't really have time or energy to defrost them properly, so you put them in a sieve and pour a little hot water through them just to take the edge off. You end up with cold berries that are soft on the edges and still a little frozen in the middle – call them 'ice berries' and it almost sounds like you made some effort. I told the 8yo they were half berry, half ice lolly. They go perfectly with the warm, fragrant apple pancakes. A great way to start the weekend.

BANANA & PEANUT BUTTER (or NUTELLA) PANCAKES

🐦 Dry: 125g *plain flour*, 1tbsp *sugar*, 1½tsp *baking powder*, ½tsp *salt*.

Wet: 115g *milk*, 1 beaten *egg*, 25g *peanut butter* (or *Nutella*), 2 mashed *bananas*.

Mix wet into dry.

Fry in *sunflower oil*. Flip when 'holes' appear & bottom golden.

Serve in a stack with optional *butter*, *maple syrup*, *bacon* or *fruit*.

👤 This final pancake recipe reminds me of a trip I took with the 8yo to California. Our last destination was San Diego, where I was taking part in a scientific conference. While in town, we hunted down the cafe with the 'best breakfast in San Diego'. We had their acclaimed Peanut Butter & Banana French Toast, and both decided it was incredible. This recipe tries to recreate it in pancake form, bringing back memories of Southern Californian sunshine, bottomless coffee and the perfect blend of travel, science, relaxation, and family time. If you don't like peanut butter, try the version with Nutella - it's great either way!

WAFFLES

Dry: 150g *SR flour*, 1tbsp *cornflour*, 1tbsp *caster sugar*, ½tsp *salt*.

Wet: 240ml warm *milk*, 25g melted *butter*, 1 *egg yolk*, 1tsp *vanilla extract*.

Slowly add wet mix into dry mix, combine.

Whisk 1 *egg white* & 1tbsp *caster sugar*. Gently fold into batter.

Leave to stand as long as you can, 10-30 min. Cook on hot waffle iron, ca. 3 min, Serve with *bacon* or *fruit* and *maple syrup*.

The 8yo would eat waffles every Saturday at *The Pig & Pastry* before lockdowns curbed his habit. Adorably, when he was 6, he once told me that he had "adopted Little Ted from the charity shop, and what adopted children need is waffles and lots of hugs". The hunt for a good waffle recipe has been a challenging mission. Separating the egg into yolk and white, whipping the white and folding it in, although being a bit of a pain, gives the lighter waffle I was searching for. This much batter will fill a standard waffle iron and make four 12cm square waffles. If you want more, double the quantities of batter (you can freeze cooked waffles and reheat them in a toaster). If you want your waffles to look 'Instagram-pretty' with ragged edges, don't completely fill the waffle iron – you avoid the mess of spilling waffle batter, and get rustic edges, like on the photograph.

BOILED EGG & MARMITE SOLDIERS

Toast 2-3 slices of *bread* per person, *butter*, spread thinly with *marmite*. Cut crusts off bread then cut into soldiers

Cook large *eggs* (1 or 2 per person) in water at rolling boil, 5 min.

Serve and get dipping!

As I've written about elsewhere in this book, Sam adored marmite, and when he was really ill, the powerful flavour it delivered from just a small amount on toast was one of the few things he could face eating. This is a weekend breakfast legacy to him that is simultaneously the best way of eating marmite and the finest way of eating boiled eggs you will ever find. The salty yeasty punch of marmite and the simple rich indulgence of a perfectly boiled egg with a soft yolk are ideally matched. Of course, marmite is... well... a marmite ingredient, but if you're one of those who love it, once you've tried this, you'll find your knife hovering over the marmite jar every time you boil an egg.

BACON & EGG SANDWICH

Lightly *butter* two slices of freshest possible *white bread*.

Fry 2 rashers good-quality *bacon*.

Fry 1 *egg* in a little sunflower oil. It is vital to keep the yolk soft.

Assemble and serve with *HP sauce* (or *ketchup* if you really must).

I know this is not a recipe, but sometimes, when you know it is going to be a long hard day, you need permission to make something like this – with this official 'recipe', I give you permission! The bacon and egg sandwich is the king of breakfast sandwiches. The bacon should be the very best quality – ideally you need dry cure back bacon from *M&K*, my local butchers, but I do understand that is probably not practical for most people! The egg should be fried with the yolk left soft, but I do like my egg 'easy over' as I really cannot abide uncooked egg white. Putting a lid on the frying pan for the last minute also 'cooks' the top of the egg white. The most controversial bit is the choice of sauce – in this house it is definitely brown. I experimented once with giving the 8yo ketchup instead – given his disgusted response, that's something I won't do again in a hurry.

FRIED CHICKEN

🐦 Cut *boneless chicken thighs* in half.

Soak all day in *milk* and a squeeze of *lemon* juice (or just *buttermilk* if you can get it), with 2tsp *paprika*, 1tsp *dried thyme*, 1 bashed *garlic* clove, *salt*, *pepper*.

Drain, then dredge in *flour* with similar *seasoning blend* (no garlic).

Deep fry, 180°C, 6 min.

👤 Fried chicken is deeply comforting and has got me through some very bad times. I swear this stuff is almost as good as what you can get from a well-known takeaway chain. Whenever we visited the USA, Sam, me and the 7yo always went to at least one KFC. I love that in the US, fried chicken is never served with fries, but with mash or mac & cheese – perfect for home cooking. Fried chicken is also great with corn, which we always grow on the allotment.

For *American 'gravy'* just make a white sauce with the *dripping* from the first batch of fried chicken (instead of butter), *flour, stock, milk, salt* & *pepper*.

Another (dirtier) way to enjoy fried chicken is to put it in a good *brioche burger bun* with *sriracha mayo* (literally just 2:1 mayo:sriracha), *jalapenos* and *shredded lettuce*. Even though the 7yo isn't a massive fan of chillies, he goes completely crazy for sriracha mayo!

CHICAGO-STYLE RIBS

 Cook

Dry rub (1tbsp *paprika*, 1tsp *celery salt*, 1tsp *brown sugar*, 1tsp *garlic powder*, ½tsp *dried thyme*, ½tsp *mustard powder*, ¼tsp *white pepper*) on *thick cut pork ribs*, leave 30 min.

Roast, Fan 200, 15 min.

Lower heat to Fan 120, wrap *ribs* in foil, place on a rack above small baking tray of *water*, 2-2.5 h (very thick ribs may need longer).

 Finish

Brush cooked ribs in BBQ sauce (170g *ketchup*, 25g *black treacle*, 25g *golden syrup*, 60ml *cider vinegar*, 60ml water, ½tsp *salt*, ½tsp *black pepper*). Stand 10 min.

Serve with extra BBQ sauce.

I love ribs. If I was on death row, (and in honesty I've sometimes felt like that since Sam passed away), the dish I would order is a huge slab of ribs, homemade slaw, and a mountain of golden lightly battered onion rings. This ribs recipe is adapted from a book I love (*Dirty Food* by *Carol Hilker*). Chicago ribs have both a dry rub and a sauce applied at the end, and it's my favourite way to have them. The recipe may be two tweets – but it's not hard, and it's worth it! It also gives you some leftover barbecue sauce. This kind of home-cooked junk food is my go-to on a Saturday. Slow-cooked perfection to eat in front of an episode of Dr Who with the 7yo.

BEER-BATTERED ONION RINGS

Add 220ml *fizzy cold beer* to 120g *plain flour* & ½tsp *salt*.

Slice *large onion* into rings, coat in seasoned flour.

Dip in batter, deep fry in batches in hot *oil* until crisp & golden.

Drain, season, serve.

I know it may seem strange to include a recipe for a simple side dish – but sometimes, one beautiful thing on a plate can elevate your whole meal to the next level – a 'hero dish'. These onion rings do that. If I have the time and energy, I cook ribs properly from scratch – you can find my favourite recipe on the previous page – but if not, these onion rings will elevate one of those slabs of pre-cooked ribs you can buy from most supermarkets. The alcohol in the beer does cook off, but if you don't want to use beer, just use fizzy ice-cold water.

Gardening was one of Sam's passions, and we have always grown onions on our allotment – they are one of the easiest and most satisfying things to grow. The photograph shows me and the 7yo planting the onion sets. The 7yo always enjoys watching their progress and helping to harvest them. Onion rings are a fantastic way to use larger onions, and (whisper it quietly) I may even prefer them to french fries.

FISH and CHIPS

 Cut large *potatoes* into chips, soak in water.

Drain & dry chips. Dredge *fish fillet* in seasoned *flour.*

Add 200ml *fizzy cold beer* to 125g *plain flour*, 1tsp *baking powder* & ½tsp *salt.*

Deep fry chips 150°C until soft, 6 min, drain.

Dip *cod fillets* in batter, deep fry 180°C, 5-8 min. Keep warm.

Finish chips, 190°C, 2-3 min.

Before lockdown, I'd never made fish and chips – but the chippy was shut, and I craved it. I tried to emulate the amazing meal we ate as a family at Stein's Fish & Chips down in Padstow. The home-made version was so good, I've done it again. I'd recommend Maris Piper potatoes and cod for the fish, but any white fish fillets will work – cooking time depends on thickness. The recipe here is easy, you just slowly crank up the temperature in the deep fat fryer as you go!

When the photo was taken, there were sadly no mushy peas. Sam's family originate from Lancashire, and always make cracking mushy peas. It takes some time, and I can never do it as well as them, so for me, opening a can is fine. It's easy to make a quick tartare, simply by putting chopped *capers, gherkins* & *parsley* through *mayo* with a squeeze of *lemon juice.*

BUFFALO & BBQ CHICKEN WINGS

 Chicken Wings

15 *wings* – discard tips, halve wings at 'elbow' to give mini drumstick & upper wing.

Mix 100g *flour*, ½tsp *paprika*, ½tsp *salt*, ½tsp *black pepper*.

Coat wings in flour, leave 30 min.

Deep fry (180°C, 7 min) & drain.

Melt 50g *butter* in 75ml *Frank's hot sauce*.

Tip wings in sauce, shake, serve.

 Sides

Slice *celery* & *carrot* into sticks.

Ranch dressing: 2tbsp *mayo*, 2tbsp *sour cream*, 2tsp *white wine vinegar*, ¼tsp *salt*, pinch *black pepper*, pinch *garlic powder*, generous fine-chopped *parsley* & *chives*.

Wings are the ultimate Saturday night TV food and bring back so many happy 'bar & baseball' memories of evenings spent with Sam on the road in America. It may seem a lot of butter, but you don't eat it all, and anyway, it's delicious and you need it with the vinegary heat of the hot sauce. To make BBQ wings, replace hot sauce with *BBQ sauce* and halve the *butter*. The 7yo is now transitioning from BBQ wings, and steals increasing numbers of the hot wings!

HOMEMADE PIZZA

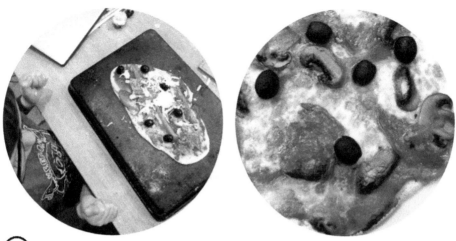

 Dough

Mix 250g *bread flour*, 250g *plain flour*, 1½tsp *salt*, 1 heaped tsp *dried yeast*.

Add 1tbsp *olive oil*, 325ml warm water, knead (I use a mixer – it's a wet dough).

Place in oiled bowl. Cover 1-2 h until risen.

Knock back. Shape ½ into 2 pizza bases on floured surface. Freeze ½.

 Topping

Open can *Mutti Pizza Sauce*.

Using a spoon spread a few spoonfuls thinly on the pizza base.

Add your favourite toppings – mine are *salami, black olives, mushrooms & mozzarella*. Scatter a little *parmesan* (or *cheddar*) over. Cook, Fan 230, 8-10 min.

We love homemade pizza night! I get all sorts of things out of the fridge and cupboards and the 7yo invents his own pizzas – it's anarchic fun. Sam was amazing at throwing parties for the 7yo and his friends after school – the most popular were always his pizza parties (sadly such parties are not in my skillset). I make no apologies for *Mutti pizza sauce*, it's the best shortcut ingredient I know. The dough is *Hugh Fearnley-Whittingstall's* 'magic dough' – it makes everything from breadsticks to loaves, and it freezes.

BEEF & ALE STEW with HORSERADISH DUMPLINGS

Toss 350g *beef shin* in *seasoned flour* – fry in *oil* till brown.

Add 330ml *ale*, 150ml *water*.

Add 1 *onion*, 2 *carrots*, 2 *celery* stalks (all thick sliced), good shake *Worcester sauce, bay leaf, thyme, salt & pepper*.

Place in casserole dish with lid, Fan 140, 3+ h.

Mix 100g *SR flour* 50g *suet*, 1tbsp *horseradish sauce*, 2-3tbsp water, shape.

Fan 180, add dumplings, 15 min. Lid off, 15 min.

When you've been for a wintry outdoor adventure, which is something I often do with the 7yo, there's nothing better than getting back to a house filled with the smell of beef & ale stew. This is a recipe the 7yo can cook some of before going out – giving him something to look forward to as we go exploring a local nature reserve. All you need to do when you get home is pop the dumplings in the top of the casserole and clean off your wellies. Do ask specifically for *shin of beef* ('*stewing steak*' on the butcher's counter in big supermarkets is often shin). It really is the best as it cooks long and slow without ever toughening up. Serve with jacket potatoes or crusty bread.

SWEET and SOUR HAGGIS

 Sweet and Sour

Fry *onion* pieces in *oil*, 2 min.

Add *red pepper*, grated *ginger*, 2 min.

Add small 225g *can pineapple chunks* & juice. Boil.

Add 1tbsp *light soy sauce*, 1tbsp *rice vinegar*, 1tsp *cornflour*.

Shape *haggis* in balls. Dip in *flour*, then batter (2:1 by wt. *beer:flour*).

Deep fry 7 min. Add to sauce, serve.

 Egg Fried Rice

Stir fry *egg* (30 sec) in *oil*.

Add cooled *boiled rice*, 1tbsp *soy sauce* and *peas*.

Fry till rice gets crisp fried bits.

I got more abuse for this recipe on Twitter than any other I have cooked. The bottom line is that in 2020, Burns night and Chinese New Year fell on the same day and I wanted to do a double celebration. It tastes amazing – the spicy haggis goes perfectly with the sweet sauce and is ideally suited to the crisp battered style of take-away sweet & sour. The 7yo adores sweet & sour, and I think this is the best one I've ever made, but if you really can't face it, just replace the haggis with pork. The sauce is adapted from a *Ching-He Huang* recipe, but it is essentially the way it's made in every UK Cantonese takeaway.

LAMB DOPIAZA, SPICED GREEN BEANS

  Lamb Dopiaza

Coat 400g *diced lamb leg* with *black pepper* (lots) & 100g *yoghurt*.
Fry 6 pods of *cardamom seeds*, 1½tsp *coriander seed*, 1½ tsp *cumin seed*. Bash with 1tsp *garam masala*, ½tsp *turmeric*.
Cut 1 *onion* into wedges, fry till brown, remove.
Fry 2 sliced *onions*, 2 cloves *garlic*, 10g *ginger*, 15 min.
Add chopped *red chilli* & spices, 1 min.
Add 1tbsp *tomato puree* & lamb, 4 min.
Add 300ml *water*, simmer, lid on, 1 h.
Reduce sauce until tender, 15 min.
Add onion wedges, ½tsp *garam masala*, serve.

 Spiced Beans

Blanch *green beans*.
Fry 1tsp *yellow mustard seed*, 5 *curry leaves*, sliced *green chilli*, 2 min.
Add 50g *desiccated coconut*, 2 min.
Add green beans, ½tsp *garam masala*, *salt*, 2 min.

Including this dish is a bit of an indulgence, not just a Saturday one, because try as I might, it's un-tweetable! But this 'Hairy Bikers' recipe is my favourite curry – packed with flavour. Sam and I used to eat curries after putting the 7yo to bed – now the 7yo is increasingly craving them himself (they grow up so fast). Going to the effort with the vegetable side dish really makes it feel 'Saturday' special.

CHICKEN KATSU CURRY

 Katsu Sauce

Rough chop 1 *onion*, gently fry in *oil* till golden, 10-15 min.
Add 1 clove sliced *garlic*, 10g chopped *ginger*, 5 min.
Add ½tbsp *Madras curry powder*, ¼tsp *turmeric*, ¼tsp *ground star anise*, *black pepper*, 2 min.
Add 10g *plain flour*, stir. Slowly add 250ml *chicken stock*, stirring.
Add 1tsp *tomato puree*, simmer 5 min.
Blend until smooth. Reheat when needed.

 Chicken

Bash two *chicken breasts* or *fillets* until flattened.
Dip in *seasoned flour*, then beaten *egg* then *panko breadcrumbs*.
Fry in 50-100ml *sunflower oil* in pan until golden (ca. 4 min per side).

Truly the gateway meal for getting kids to love curry. Katsu Curry is mild, tasty and the crispy chicken is a sure-fire winner. Ever since he was very small, the 8yo has loved it – look at that 2yo hand in the photo – he couldn't wait to eat it! Serve the sauce on the side and kids can dip the sliced crispy chicken into it as much (or as little) as they want. Something acidic on the side is nice – Japanese pickles from a jar are ideal. Although the sauce takes a little time, it can be made in advance and reheated when needed, so getting dinner on the table is very fast. You can always scale up the sauce and freeze some. Serve with simple steamed rice with a sprinkle of *Shichimi Togarashi*.

CHIPOTLE CHILLI CON CARNE

Chop 4 rashers *streaky bacon*. Fry in casserole, set aside.

Season 400g diced *beef shin* (stewing steak) with *salt & pepper*, brown in casserole, remove.

Fry 1 diced *onion*, 5 min.

Add ½ diced *red pepper*, 1 sliced *garlic* clove, 5 min.

Add 1tsp *cumin*, 1tsp *unsweetened cocoa powder*, 1 min.

Add browned beef, 1-2tsp *chipotle chilli flakes*, 400g can *chopped tomatoes*, ½ can water, 1 *bay leaf*, bring to boil.

Lid on, Fan 140, 2.5 h.

Add 1 drained can *red kidney beans* & fried bacon, 30 min.

A luxury Mexican-style chilli for a winter Saturday – perfect after a long cold walk. You can always replace the 2.5 h in the oven with a day in the slow cooker if you want a really long walk! In Mexico, chilli is often made with diced rather than minced meat. Shin of beef gives the tenderest, chunkiest chilli you will ever taste. I am cooking for the 8yo, so I hold back a bit on the chilli, if you want more, then add chopped red chillies with the cumin. The quantities here are enough for 2-3 hungry people – I get some leftovers for a jacket potato the following day. Serve it up with *rice*, *sour cream*, and extra *red chillies*.

PRETZEL ROLLS

 Preparing (makes 6)

Mix 450g *plain flour*, 5g *dried yeast*, 1½tsp *salt*, 2tsp *sugar*, 40g melted *butter*, 260ml water.

Knead to smooth dough. Prove, covered, in oiled bowl, 1 h.

Knock back, shape into six 125g rolls on lined baking sheet.

Cover, leave to rise, 30 min.

 Baking

Boil ⅓-filled large pan of water. Carefully add 50g bicarbonate of soda (it fizzes). Poach buns, 30 sec on each side. With a slotted spoon, lift buns back onto lined baking sheet.

Brush with beaten *egg*, sprinkle *sea salt*, with sharp knife gently mark 'X' (or other shape) on top.

Bake, Fan 200, ca. 25 min.

Sam adored pretzels. I think it was partly a salt thing – cystic fibrosis patients have an imbalance in salt levels and can crave salty food as a result. He loved these pretzel rolls – satisfying to bake, and surprisingly easy for a spectacular finish. The bicarbonate boil gives them their gorgeous colour. Speaking chemically, it raises the pH and means the Maillard reaction (which causes things to brown on baking) works super-fast! The recipe is adapted from *Carol Hilker*'s book *Dirty Food*. These awesome rolls are as good with a bowl of soup or stew as they are stuffed full of pulled pork or brisket. Make them!

PULLED PORK

🐦 Mix 2tsp *smoked paprika*, 2tsp *cumin*, 2tsp *black pepper*, 2tsp *brown sugar*, 1tsp *salt*. Rub into ca. 1kg *pork shoulder*.

Put 1 sliced *onion* & 1 *sage leaf*, in slow cooker, place pork on top, add 150ml *India Pale Ale* & 50ml *cider vinegar*.

Slow cook, 6 h (or in casserole, Fan 130, 4 h, add *water* if needed).

Remove pork, 'pull' into shreds with two forks.

Skim fat off liquid, strain, add 3tbsp to 150ml *good barbecue sauce*.

Mix sauce through pork.

👤 So easy, so tasty – put everything in a slow cooker, leave it for the day and come back to delicious pulled pork. I have suggested using a medium pork shoulder, which will generously serve 4-6, but would serve 2 with *lots* of leftovers! You can scale the recipe easily – just use less/more rub & sauce. This pairs perfectly with Pretzel Rolls (page 143) & Homemade Slaw (page 145). If you put all three together, it's a lot of effort, but makes for a lovely cooking-filled Saturday and a great sense of satisfaction. You can buy good barbecue sauce, but if you are going for it, you should make your own (170g *ketchup*, 25g *black treacle*, 25g *golden syrup*, 60ml *cider vinegar*, 60ml water, ½tsp *salt*, ½tsp *black pepper*).

HOMEMADE SLAW

 Very finely slice ½ *small white cabbage*, 1-2 *carrots*, ¼ *red onion*.

Add 2tbsp *mayo*, 2tbsp *sour cream*, 1-2tbsp *cider vinegar*, 1tsp *sugar*, 1tsp *celery seed*, ½tsp salt, pinch *garlic powder*, *black pepper*.

Mix. Leave to stand in fridge, 30 min.

I love slaw! It's exactly what I want on the side of pulled pork, fried chicken, burgers, or in fact any of the home-cooked 'junk food' you can find in these books. The crunchiness and acidity combine to cut through the Saturday indulgence and at least help you feel you've got a few vegetables inside you, even if they might be coated in mayo & sour cream. Sam and I always used to argue about slaw – he said the vegetables should be cut ultra-thin with a mandolin, while I preferred to use my Japanese chef's knife, which gives a slightly thicker slaw. Looking back, I wonder why we wasted all those words, but equally, arguments like that are a vital part of the fabric of married life.

For variation, *fennel*, *red cabbage*, *beansprouts*, or *apple* are excellent additions or replacements. The *celery seed* can be replaced with other fragrant flavourings like *caraway seed*, chopped *rosemary* or *sesame seed*. A dash of *mustard* or *wasabi* can lift the slaw. Finally, swapping the vinegar to *white wine vinegar* makes a sharper slaw, while *rice vinegar* (and 1tsp *soy sauce*) can send it in an Asian direction.

SLOW-COOKED TEXAS-STYLE BRISKET

Mix 1tbsp *chilli powder*, 1tbsp *salt*, 2tsp *black pepper*, 2tsp *brown sugar*, 1tsp *garlic powder*, 1tsp *mustard powder*, 1tsp *cayenne pepper*, ½tsp *dried oregano*, 1 crushed *bay leaf*, rub into 1kg beef brisket.

Roast, Fan 160, 30 min.

Add 250ml beef stock, then water to 1.5cm depth in tin. Cover in foil.

Roast turning twice, Fan 130, 2-3 h (until fork tender).

Slice and serve with the roasting juices.

This recipe gives a lovely, spiced crust on the brisket – you then carve it into thin slices and serve with some of the roasting juices. It's great in a hot sandwich, but also nice with American-style veggies like roasted sweet potatoes, pumpkins, sweetcorn, or peppers. This approach to cooking brisket is versatile – you can change the rub to North African spices or Mediterranean herbs. You can also throw in some veggies that survive casserole-style cooking with the beef when you wrap it in foil, giving a whole meal in one parcel. Like pulled pork, this is great cooking for a crowd (1kg brisket will serve 4-6) – make Pretzel rolls, slow roast the meat, make slaw, and all dig in while you play board games. Sam was the one who organised our social life – he was the extrovert; I am the introvert. I miss throwing parties like that but as a single dad, it's just so hard to have the energy.

MEATBALLS and BROAD BEANS

 Meatballs

Mix 250g *beef mince*, 50g *panko*, fine-chopped small *onion & garlic clove*, 1 tbsp each chopped *parsley, mint & dill*, 1 tsp chopped *capers*, 1 tsp *cumin*, ½tsp *coriander*, ½tsp grated *nutmeg*, ½tsp salt, pinch each *cinnamon, ground clove, allspice & pepper*.
Add ½ beaten egg, shape into meatballs.
Fry in olive oil until brown, Remove.

 Beans and Assembly

Blanch 250g *broad beans*, 2 min. Drain, cool, remove skins from half.
Put 2tbsp *olive oil* in meatball pan, fry 3 sprigs *thyme*, 2 sliced *garlic cloves*, 5 sliced *spring onions*, 3 min.
Add skin-on beans, 1 tbsp *lemon juice*, 50ml *chicken stock*, 10 min.
Add meatballs, 300ml *stock*, cover, simmer 25 min.
Add *extra herbs*, squeeze *lemon juice*, skin-off beans, serve.

Kids love meatballs but are less convinced by broad beans. We grow them on our allotment, and the 8yo loves to pick and pod them, which is half the battle won! This (believe-it-or-not) simplified *Ottolenghi* recipe serves 2. It's a fragrantly herbal way to eat meatballs and a tasty way to use a broad bean glut – serve it with *rice* or *flat-breads*. It gives your spice cupboard a workout, but it's not hard. Removing half the beans from their inner skin to reveal the bright green, jewel-like heart looks good and gives two textures.

'CHINESE' DUCK with POTATO PANCAKES

 Duck

Prick skin of *whole duck*, rub with 2tsp crushed *Szechuan peppercorns* & generous *salt*.

Roast on wire rack in tray, Fan 180, 25min. Pour off fat.

Then roast, Fan 100, 75 min. Pour off most of fat.

Pour 125g *runny honey* over duck.

Roast, Fan 160, 15 min, baste with pan juices. On final baste, add 75ml *soy sauce*.

Remove, rest, serve with pan juices.

 Pancakes

Mix 250g cold dry *mashed potato*, 75g *flour*, 1tsp *baking powder*.

Whisk 125ml *milk* & 2 *eggs*. Add to potato mix. Stir.

Fry spoonfuls of batter in *sunflower oil* until golden brown, 2-3 min per side. Keep warm in oven.

This adapted *Tom Kerridge* recipe is lovely weekend cooking and makes a great alternative to a roast dinner. It does take some effort (hidden in the wording is the fact you must make dry mashed potatoes in order to make the pancakes), but it is utterly delicious. This is great with peas or braised lettuce, I like to combine the two and serve it with Petits Pois a la Française (see page 171). This is the kind of thing I cooked for Sam on special occasions.

HAM HOCK and SAVOY CABBAGE

 Ham hock

Coat *ham hock* (ca. 600g) in *olive oil*, roast, Fan 160, 30 min.
Gently fry 1 rough-chopped *onion*, 1 thick-sliced *carrot*, 1 sliced *celery stick* and 1 smashed *garlic* clove in *olive oil*.
Add 100ml *white wine*, reduce 50%.
Add 1 litre *chicken stock*, 1 *star anise*, 3 *cloves*, ½ *cinnamon stick* and ham hock, simmer 1.5-2 h until tender.

 Dressing, Cabbage, Finishing

Mix 4tbsp *olive oil*, 1tbsp *lemon juice*, 1tbsp *red wine vinegar*, 1tsp *Dijon mustard*, *salt* & *pepper*.
Cut *savoy cabbage* in ribbons, blanch in salted boiling water, 4 min, drain.
Take chunks of meat off ham hock, add to cabbage in pan, add dressing and 50ml *ham cooking water*. Stir, warm, serve.

This is a delicious, relaxing, slow Saturday afternoon cook. It is adapted and simplified from a *Spuntino* recipe to ensure the ingredient list is manageable in tweet form without losing the heart of the dish. The soft meat, vibrant cabbage and sharp dressing are a fabulous combination. It just needs serving with plenty of crusty bread to mop up the juices.

BEER CAN CHICKEN and HOMEMADE BBQ SAUCE

 Chicken

Open *tall can American beer*, drink 150ml.

Mix 2tsp *paprika*, 2tsp *light brown sugar*, 2tsp *salt*, 1tsp *celery salt*, 1tsp *dried oregano*, 1tsp *mustard powder*, 1tsp *black pepper*, 1tsp *ground cumin*, 1tsp *garlic powder*, 1tsp *chilli powder*.

Rub *large chicken* with 2-3tbsp of dry rub.

Place 2 sprigs *rosemary* in beer can, place chicken onto can so it is standing up. Stand in roasting tin.

Roast, Fan 200, ca. 1 h, until cooked (or cook on large BBQ with a lid).

 BBQ Sauce

Gently fry ¼ chopped *onion* & 1 chopped clove *garlic* in 1tbsp *sunflower oil*.

Add 100g *ketchup*, 100ml *cider vinegar*, 1tbsp *American mustard*, 1tbsp *light brown sugar*, 1tsp *Worcester sauce*, simmer 10 min.

This is a fun, flavoursome way to cook chicken. It's a *Paula Deen* classic of Southern States US cooking. Any recipe that starts with drinking beer is a winner! It can be barbecued, I almost put it in the next section – but you need a big barbecue with a lid! The chicken roasts from the outside and steams with the beer from the inside, giving delicious crunchy skin and soft yielding flesh. To serve, add salads, sides, and good homemade BBQ sauce. The dry rub quantities are enough for two chickens – it will keep in an airtight container.

BARBECUES

THE MAGIC OF BARBECUE

There is nothing better than a hot sunny day, with a fine spread of food laid out on a table in the garden, or in our case, back yard. My own family doesn't have a tradition of barbecuing. Other than camping trips, I don't recall ever cooking outdoors with my parents. However, for Sam's family, the barbecue is a 'big deal'. The gathering of the whole family for an outdoor feast is a fixture of summer weekends. The 8yo will play with his cousins, Sam's dad will bustle round the barbecue, and his mum will produce incredible side dishes from

the kitchen. The table groans with food, everyone talks over the top of everybody else, drinks are poured, stories & jokes are shared, and it's just the most fun. Having grown up with this, Sam was passionate about the importance of outdoor cooking & eating, and it was something I was delighted to incorporate into our own family life.

This section illustrates our family approach to the barbecue. It contains some classic meat & fish dishes, as well as vegetarian options and some stand-out side dishes. The secret of a good barbecue is to have a few things on the table that really make it special – as you will see, these can be very easy to put together, but with minimal effort, they elevate the whole experience, moving it far beyond shop-bought burgers & sausages and a bagged salad.

In terms of barbecue cooking, it is vital to let the initial blast of heat die down, otherwise you just cremate everything. Wait until the coals are coated in white ash and the flames have gone. Another good tip is to load your coals asymmetrically in the barbecue – this gives a hot side, and a cooler side. This means you can move food to the cooler side once it is cooked, or if the coals get a bit feisty. Of course, you can do far fancier things with indirect heat on barbecues, and with smokers, but all the recipes here can be cooked on a typical simple family barbecue. If the weather fails you, then they can just be cooked on a hot griddle pan in the kitchen instead.

PROFESSOR DAVE's BARBECUE BURGER

🐦 Mix 250g *minced beef* (10%+ fat), ¼ fine-diced small *red onion*, handful *panko*, 1tsp *ground coriander*, ½tsp *ground cumin*, *salt*, *pepper*.

Add ½ *beaten egg*. Shape into patties, chill.

Barbecue (or griddle), add slice *cheese* & cover with a lid for last 2 min.

Serve in *brioche bun* with fried sliced *mushrooms* & *BBQ sauce*.

👤 It's essential to have a good burger recipe for the perfect barbecue and I've spent a lot of time on this one. I love these burgers with a hint of spice – it enhances the flavour but does not dominate. You can leave out the cumin & coriander for a great, more traditional burger. The recipe makes 2 very large burgers, 3 medium burgers or 4 child-sized burgers. The secrets are: (i) to avoid the burgers being dry, don't use 'extra lean' minced beef; (ii) add panko breadcrumbs, they hold onto the fat and stop the burger drying out; (iii) don't add too much egg, just enough to bind. If you are going to the effort of homemade burgers, you must serve them on a very good brioche burger bun (supermarkets sell them but there is also a recipe on page 204). For barbecue sauce, I really like *Red's Kansas City Style*, but you will find your own favourite, or use the recipe on page 150.

HALLOUMI BURGER with BEETROOT DRESSING

Slice block *halloumi* into two thin slices, trim to size of roll, rub with *olive oil*.

Peel & grate 1 large *beetroot*. Mix with 100g *natural yoghurt*, 1tbsp *white wine vinegar*, 6 chopped *mint* leaves, *salt* & *pepper*.

Barbecue/griddle halloumi 3-4 min per side, turning 90° for pattern.

Put in *brioche bun*, top with beetroot relish.

Why shouldn't vegetarians have delicious burgers to eat. I'm not a massive fan of vegetarian dishes that pretend to be meat – I understand why vegetarians like them, but as someone who eats meat, I can never really see the point. If I'm having vegetarian food, I want it to be unique – making the very most of its non-meat origins. This is an adapted *Nigel Slater* recipe that is one of our favourites. In honesty, I have changed just one thing. He makes this burger with feta, but I struggled to griddle it effectively – the moisture content is just too high. I replaced the feta with halloumi and this tasty burger was born. *Nigel*'s beetroot relish is delicious – I didn't change a thing about that. Just like any burger, you should serve this up on a good quality brioche roll. It's always a nice touch to grill the open faces of the roll to give it a bit of colour and texture.

HAKE, LEMON and HERBS

 Place 2 *hake fillets* on kitchen foil.

On one fillet, place thin *lemon* slices, very thin *fennel* slices, chopped herbs (e.g. *parsley, dill) salt, pepper* & *olive oil* (or *butter*).

Place second fillet on top of first, flesh sides together, wrap tightly in foil. Leave to marinade, 30 min.

Barbecue foil parcel 5-10 min (depends on size of fish & heat of grill).

This dish was prepared by Sam at his very last family barbecue and was a genuine showstopper. He bought the spectacular hake you see in the photograph from Leeds City Markets to feed about ten people as the centrepiece of a barbecue feast at his parents' house. Sam loved nothing more than cooking for family, and I like to think you can see the love he had for his family in the photo!

You can easily do something similar with more ordinary-sized fish fillets. All the flavour gets packed into the fish within the parcel. This is a great general approach for cooking any fragile fish on a barbecue – for example, salmon is fantastic barbecued in a parcel with soy sauce, mirin, lime juice, ginger, and spring onions. The parcel locks in the flavour, prevents the fish from sticking to the grill, protects it from the direct heat, and makes for easy serving. If it rains, cook the parcels at Fan 180 for 10-20 min.

WATERMELON and HALLOUMI

Mix 2 cubed large wedges *watermelon*, 150g halved *cherry tomatoes*, 2 *spring onions*, small handful *coriander*, ½ *red chilli* (optional) & 1tbsp *olive oil*. Chill

Rub *ciabatta* slices with *olive oil*, barbecue/griddle.

Slice block *halloumi* in two thin slices, rub with *olive oil*, barbecue/griddle.

Load grilled ciabatta with melon salsa, top with halloumi.

This is a *Nigel Slater* recipe and is one of the most delicious things you will ever eat on a hot summer afternoon. The cool crisp salad, the chewy grilled ciabatta, the salty warm barbecued halloumi – it's perfect and simply could not be improved. Our little back yard catches the afternoon and evening sun. I made this for the 8yo (who was 5 or 6 at the time) one glorious afternoon. I was enjoying a glass or two of chilled white wine, he was in and out of the paddling pool, which makes the whole thing less relaxed than it probably sounds! Watermelon is possibly the 8yo's very favourite thing to eat, so this dish is his idea of summer heaven.

CHICKEN TIKKA KEBABS

🐦 Mix 1 crushed *garlic* clove, 1tbsp *tikka spice mix*, 1tbsp *lemon juice* & 1tbsp *olive oil* in 100ml *natural yoghurt*.

Cube 4 boneless *chicken thighs* and marinade in yoghurt mix for 1 h.

Thread onto skewers with slices of *red pepper* (*onion* is also good).

Barbecue until chicken is cooked, 5-10 min.

Serve with *mint/yoghurt* dressing, *Indian chutneys*, *salads*, and *flatbreads*.

👤 Kebabs are a great option on the barbecue – kids love them, and you can tailor what you put on them to the specific tastes of your family. I prefer to use chicken thighs to chicken breast as they have a higher fat content, which means they are less likely to dry out. They also (in my opinion) have much better flavour. It's worth buying metal skewers that you can re-use, but when you turn them, remember they get very hot!

BLACKBERRY & APPLE SALAD

Salad: ¼ *red cabbage* & ¼ *red onion* both finely sliced, 75g *baby spinach leaves* sliced, 1 small *apple* cut into matchsticks, 100g *blackberries*, 20g toasted *hazelnuts*, 1 tsp toasted *caraway seeds*.

Dressing: 4 tbsp *olive oil*, 2 tbsp *cider vinegar*, 1 tbsp *maple syrup*, 1 tsp *Dijon mustard*.

Mix and serve.

So often, all the attention at barbecues is focussed on what's on the grill – the quality of the meat, the marinades, and the sauces. However, one of the best ways of making your barbecue extra special is to have a signature salad on the table and then just barbecue something simple, but high quality, as an accompaniment. This fantastic barbecue salad, adapted from a *Diana Henry* recipe, is perfect for this approach. It relies on the classic late summer combination of blackberry & apple, placing them on a slaw-style base. It's crunchy, tasty and with all that fruit and a maple mustard dressing is pretty much guaranteed to encourage kids to enjoy salad too – the 8yo completely demolished it! Once you've put your 'effort' into making this unique salad, all you need to do is serve it with some simply barbecued top-quality butcher's sausages & crusty bread. You are pretty much guaranteed a barbecue to remember, and you will be relaxed enough to enjoy a drink and a chat with friends and family.

ALLOTMENT SALAD

Slice 2 *courgettes*, brush with *olive oil*, barbecue/griddle.

Boil podded *broad beans*, 3 min. Cool. Remove bright green hearts from outer skin.

Mix courgettes, beans, *watercress*, crumbled *feta*, chopped *mint*.

Dress with 2 tbsp *olive oil*, 1 tbsp *lemon* juice, 1 tsp *grain mustard*, *salt & pepper*.

A simple salad made with courgettes & broad beans brought home from the allotment and eaten in the garden. We had this with an over-chilled glass of white wine when Sam had been on a bread-making course, and I had been working on the allotment. For full disclosure, I must confess that I would struggle to get the 8yo to eat this. He'd prefer it if I replaced the feta with *mozzarella*, swapped the bitter watercress for sweeter *lamb's lettuce* and maybe used some *honey* in the lemon mustard dressing to sweeten it. Bizarrely (based on what most kids like) he would also love some *marinated olives* scattered through. This is how I tend to think about adapting dishes for the 8yo. I think about his favourite things and try to incorporate some of them – this gives him a 'comfort zone' and means a dish can be a jumping-off point for him to try other things he may be less comfortable with, potentially expanding his palate.

SIMPLE BARBECUE SIDE SALADS

 Tomato Salad

Slice 3-4 good quality *tomatoes*, arrange on small plate.
Sprinkle ½tsp *caster sugar*, pinch of *salt*.
Add finely chopped ¼ *red onion* and small handful *capers*.
Drizzle 1tbsp *olive oil*.

 Quick Pickled Cucumber

Cut ½ deseeded *cucumber* into half-moons.
Soak in 25ml *white wine vinegar*, 25ml *water* & 1tbsp *caster sugar*,
30 min.
Drain & serve.

 Watermelon Salad.

Cut *watermelon* into cubes.
Toss with handful chopped *mint*.
Dress (optional) with: 1tbsp *olive oil*, 1tbsp *lemon* juice, 1tsp *caster
sugar*, ½tsp grated *ginger* (optional).

Celeriac Remoulade
Chop ½ small *celeriac* into finest matchsticks possible.
Dress with 3tbsp *mayo*, 1tbsp *lemon juice*, 1tsp *Dijon mustard*, ½tsp *caster sugar*, *salt* & *pepper*.
Leave to stand in fridge, 30 min.

 Beetroot, Sour Cream & Horseradish.
Cut 2-3 *cooked beetroot* into cubes.
Mix 2tbsp *sour cream* with 1tsp *horseradish sauce*.
Stir beetroot into cream sauce.

 Caprese Salad.
Slice 2-3 good quality *tomatoes*. Season with *salt* & *pepper*.
Tear ½ *mozzarella* into chunks scatter over.
Add small *basil* leaves.
Drizzle 1tbsp *olive oil*.

Every barbecue needs a salad, but sometimes it's tempting to do little more than reach for a bag of salad or chop up some lettuce & cucumber and put out a bottle of salad cream. The ideas given above are not elaborate, but they are fast and tasty and will bring something different and colourful to your barbecue table. I think that certain salads marry well with certain dishes. For example, barbecued oily fish, like mackerel, just cries out for a tomato salad, or something acidic like pickled cucumber. Smoked fish, sausages or gammon are a perfect match with celeriac remoulade. Barbecued steaks are moved to the next level with beetroot, sour cream, and horseradish. Experiment with these salads and find out what your flavour preferences are. Try to marry up flavours to make your individual dishes come together on the plate into a delicious meal, using just one or two well-chosen simple salads to make your barbecue more special.

LAMB CHOPS with TAHINI CUCUMBER SALAD

 Mix 2tbsp *tahini*, 2tbsp *natural yoghurt*, juice of 1 *lemon*, 1 crushed clove *garlic*, 1tbsp *olive oil*, *salt & pepper*. Add 1-3tbsp *water* to give desired consistency.

Chop ½ deseeded *cucumber* in half-moons. Dress cucumber with tahini sauce, scatter crumbled *feta* (optional) chopped *dill & mint*.

Rub *lamb chops* in *olive oil*, *thyme* leaves, *salt & pepper*.

Barbecue, ca. 3-4 min per side. Using tongs hold fat on grill to render.

This was the last barbecue I cooked at home for Sam. It might seem luxury to fire up the barbecue just to cook some chops, but it's very much the way we roll(ed). A barbecue should not always be about cooking as much as possible on the grill, it's about the flavour you can get into food by cooking it on fire. These lamb chops came from our local butcher, *M&K Butchers*, and simply cooked on the barbecue, they were just incredible – one of the tastiest things I have ever eaten. We served this with some homemade flatbreads also cooked on the barbecue. You can find the recipe on page 212, but instead of frying the flattened dough in the final step, just place it straight down on the barbecue – the flatbreads puff up and char beautifully.

BARBECUED HOT DOGS

🐦 Slice 1 *onion*, gently fry in *sunflower oil* until golden brown.

Barbecue *good hot dog sausages* until cooked & slightly charred.

Serve in the best roll you can – ideally a *brioche hot dog roll*.

Add *French's yellow mustard* & *Heinz tomato ketchup*.

👤 Hot dogs take me right back to one of my happiest afternoons – sitting with Sam watching baseball at the San Francisco Giants in the blazing afternoon sunshine, with a fabulous view out over the bay. We gorged on junk food – nachos, hot dogs, the works – and enjoyed a game in which the Giants had a great come-from-behind victory against the Philadelphia Phillies. This was the season that the Giants went on, a month or so later, to win the World Series. Sam wasn't really a fan of sport at all, but he loved baseball – sitting in a bar with great food, plenty of beer and a ball game on was one of our favourite ways to spend an evening in America. That afternoon sits in my memory like a blazing star – every time I taste a hot dog done perfectly, with care and love, I'm there.

SUNDAY ROASTS

THE HEARTBEAT OF FAMILY LIFE

Roast dinners have been the heartbeat of my family life since I was a child. A roast dinner forces everyone to slow down, it builds a sense of togetherness. So many of my own family memories revolve around Sunday lunch. There was always the anticipation of which meat and sauce we were going to have. My dad sat at the table, carving the meat, while mum bustled round in the kitchen making the gravy. I can even remember running off once the meal was complete to watch Space 1999 on the TV – the start of a life-long sci-fi obsession!

I serve a roast dinner on a big platter. What you see in the photographs is just the first plateful. What you don't see is how the meal goes on, with me and the 7yo stealing our favourite bits off the platter – an extra roast potato (or three), another spoonful of cabbage, a second helping of meat. Proper, greedy, interactive family eating. When Sam was here, part of our Sunday roast tradition was that as he carved, the 7yo would sneak in and Sam would give him the best offcuts. I had to pretend I was busy at the cooker and couldn't see – it was their 'secret' game. In moments like these, families are made.

When cooking a roast, I choose the vegetables depending on the meat and the season. I think certain vegetables go particularly well with certain roasts. I have tried to capture that through this chapter, which is essentially a series of individual dishes – each condensed into a single tweet. Mix and match them to make your own perfect roast.

As you read, you will see that I always make gravy from roasting pan juices to essentially the same formula – pour off excess fat, add flour, water/juices/stock/wine, season and add something acidic. Dropping the pH just a little bit always makes a sauce more lip-smacking – you can never quite take the chemist out of the cook!

I must credit Simon and Matthew, the Bishy Road butchers, who consistently supply us with top quality, locally sourced meat. We are only a small family; buying meat from them means we always get the perfectly-sized joint for a greedy Sunday roast, with just the right amount of extras for leftovers.

There are two constants on every roast dinner I cook – roast potatoes & Yorkshire puddings. I therefore start with those before considering each different meat in turn.

 Roast Potatoes

Peel & cut *potatoes* into 2-4 pieces, with flat edges & corners (King Edwards are best, Maris Piper good, we grow amazing Blue Danube).
Parboil in salted water until just starting to soften, 8-10 min.
Drain, put back on heat to dry, shake well to roughen.
Toss in *sunflower oil*.
Roast, Fan 180, 50-60 min, turning once or twice.

 Olive oil does not cook hot enough to make great roasties, and while some swear by duck/goose fat (and it does crisp beautifully), I personally find it a bit greasy tasting.

 Yorkshire Puddings (makes 5-6)

Make batter: ½ mug *plain flour*, 1 *egg*, ½ mug *milk:water* (50:50), pinch of *salt* & *white pepper*.
Heat *sunflower oil* in muffin tin (not Yorkshire Pudding tin).
Add batter.
Bake, Fan 180, 35 min, turn oven up to Fan 210 for last 10-15 min (once meat is removed).

 I know some say Yorkshire Puddings should only go with roast beef, but they are simply too good not to have more often. Using half milk half water rather than just milk lightens the batter and guarantees you that perfect rise and crisp edges.

ROAST PORK

 Meat

Leg of Pork – Fan 180, 30-35 min per 500g, then Fan 200, 20 min.

Belly Pork – Put in roasting tin with 200 ml white wine, all wrapped in foil, Fan 140, 2-3 h, then Fan 200, 20-30 min unwrapped.

Crackling – Dry pork skin, season with lots of *salt & pepper* (*fennel seeds* are good too). If it hasn't crackled (often it won't on a small joint), cut off, put back in oven in enamel tin, Fan 210 (with Yorkshire Puddings). If it still won't crackle, put under hot grill, 2 min.

 Vegetables

Roast fennel – cut in wedges, coat in *olive oil & lemon juice*, season. Roast, Fan 180, 25 min.

Braised red cabbage – slice ½ *red cabbage*, add 1 diced peeled *cooking apple*, 1tbsp *redcurrant jelly*, 1tbsp *red wine vinegar*, 20g butter 75ml *water*, simmer 1h.

 Gravy

Pour xs fat off roasting tin, add 1tbsp *flour*, stir, add ½ glass *white wine*, reduce, add *water*, stir, *season*, finish with squeeze *lemon juice*.

 Sauce

Apple sauce – 1 *cooking apple*, 2tsp *sugar*, *water*, boil.

This was Sam's favourite roast and is also the 7yo's. Pork *must* have its skin on – without crackling, roast pork is sad.

ROAST BEEF

 Meat

Topside/Silverside – Fan 180, 15-20 min per 500g + 20 min.
Rib – Fan 210, 20 min, then reduce to Fan 160, 15 min per 500g.
Season your *beef* really well with *salt* and plenty of *black pepper*.

 Vegetables

Roast beetroot & balsamic – peel and cut into wedges, place on foil, add *olive oil, balsamic vinegar, thyme, salt & pepper*. Wrap. Roast, Fan 180, 50-60 min, unwrap and finish with a little *balsamic vinegar*.
Broad beans & bacon – pod, briefly boil, cool, remove outer pale green shells, briefly fry bright green insides in *olive oil* with fried *chopped bacon*.

 Gravy

Pour some of the excess fat off roasting tin, add 1 tbsp *flour*, stir, add *water*, stir, add juices from carved beef, season with *salt & generous black pepper*, finish with a dash of *balsamic vinegar*.

 Sauce

Horseradish sauce – from jar. I tried making it once, but it was awful!
Mustard – Dijon or freshly-made Colman's English.

As a kid growing up, roast beef was definitely my favourite – two reasons: horseradish sauce is just the best, and it was the only time we were allowed Yorkshire Puddings.

ROAST LAMB

 Meat

Leg – Fan 180, 20-25 min per 500g + 20 min.
Shoulder – Fan 150, 40 min per 500g wrapped in foil, then Fan 200, 20 min unwrapped.
Breast – Fan 140, 2-3 h, wrapped in foil, then Fan 180, 30 min unwrapped.

 Vegetables

Roast Parsnip – peel & slice into long wedges, coat in *sunflower oil*, roast with potatoes, Fan 180, 50-60 min. The thin end should be crisp, bitter & almost burnt, the fat end fudgy & sweet.
Asparagus & peas – simply boiled (3 min).
Buttered leeks – slice thinly, gently fry with generous *butter*, *salt* & *pepper* until soft.

 Gravy

Pour excess fat off roasting tin, add 1tbsp *flour*, stir, add *water*, stir, add juices from carved lamb, *season*, add ½tbsp *redcurrant jelly* and finish with a dash of *balsamic vinegar*.

 Sauce

Mint relish – chopped *mint*, fine chopped *shallot*, 2tsp *caster sugar*, juice of ½ *lemon*, 1tbsp warm *water*. The sauce described here is a thin relish, if you prefer a thicker mint sauce or jelly, buy one.

ROAST CHICKEN

 Meat

Season whole *chicken* well with *salt* and *pepper*, dot skin with *butter*. Stuff with 20g *butter*, wedges of *lemon*, 2 cloves *garlic* and chopped *tarragon*. Roast, Fan 180, 20 min per 500g + 20 min. Baste 2-3 times.

 Vegetables

Steamed cabbage – melt large knob of *butter* in pan, add ½ *shredded cabbage*, and 2tbsp *water*, place lid on, steam 5 min until soft and buttery. Season.

Grandma's Green Beans – just how my Mum cooks them (I always call them 'Grandma's green beans for the 7yo). Make a simple white sauce with *butter, flour, milk, salt & white pepper*, lightly boil sliced *runner beans*, drain, pour white sauce over and heat through.

 Gravy

Pour xs fat off roasting tin, add 1tbsp *flour*, stir, add ½ glass *white wine*, reduce, add *water*, stir, *season*, finish with squeeze *lemon* juice.

 Sauce

Bread sauce (for special occasions) – heat 10g *butter*, fry 50g *onion*, *thyme*, 2 crushed *cloves*, *bay leaf* & a pinch of *salt*. Add 10g chopped *streaky bacon*. Add 150ml *milk*, simmer. Add 1 slice *white bread* ripped up. Stir & simmer until smooth.

ROAST DUCK

 Meat

Prick the *duck* skin all over with a fork, season generously with *salt & pepper*. Roast in tin on rack, Fan 180, 20 min per 500g + 20 min.

 Vegetables

Petits Pois a la Francaise – soften sliced *spring onions* in *butter*, add *frozen peas*, 100ml *chicken stock* & shredded *little gem lettuce*. Finish with a knob of *butter*, *salt* & *pepper*.

 Gravy

Pour excess fat off roasting tin, add 1 tbsp *flour*, stir, add *water*, stir, add juices from carved duck, season with *salt* & *pepper* and finish with *lemon* juice.

 Sauce

Cherry sauce – Soak 75g dried *cherries* in 200ml *red wine*. Add 1 tbsp *red wine vinegar*, 25g *sugar*. Simmer 30-60 min and reduce right down to a sticky glossy sauce (add a splash water if you go too far).

My favourite roast – definitely for high days & holidays in this house. I always associate duck with luxury, because this is what we used to have for Christmas Dinner when I was young. The cherry sauce is a *Delia Smith* recipe and is absolutely incredible – I can't eat roast duck without it!

INDIAN ROAST LAMB

 Meat

Marinade *half leg of lamb* in 200ml *yoghurt*, 6 pods worth of crushed *cardamom seeds*, 2tsp *paprika*, 2tsp *turmeric*, 2 cloves crushed *garlic*, *salt* & *pepper* for 3+ hours, cook as usual (page 169).

Indian-Spiced Potatoes and Yorkshire puddings

As page 166, but after parboiling, toss in *sunflower oil* with 1tsp *turmeric*, 1tsp *paprika*, 1tsp *cumin*. Roast as usual. Add sliced *onion* for last 15 min. Sensational! I often use them as a side dish. For YPs add *garam masala* (1tsp heaped per 5 YPs) to batter.

Vegetables

Carrots – boil, drain, add *butter* & toasted crushed *coriander seed*.
Aubergine & Feta – cube, toss in olive oil. Roast, Fan 180, 20 min, add chopped *feta* & *cherry tomatoes*, roast additional 10 min.

Gravy

Drain excess fat from spiced pan juices, add 1tbsp *flour*, heat 1 min, add *water*, stir, add dash *balsamic vinegar*, *season*.

Sauce

Mint yoghurt - chopped *mint* in *yoghurt*.

I'm not one for messing about with a Sunday Roast, but this is great, showcasing how spices can elevate a British classic.

CAKES and PUDDINGS

7yo's BLACKBERRY & APPLE CRUMBLE

 Peel, core & chop 2 *cooking apples*.

Add 1-2tbsp *sugar*. Add 2 handfuls *blackberries*.

Rub 120g *flour* and 70g *butter*. Add 60g *sugar* and mix gently.

Put fruit in small tin. Put crumble mix on top.

Bake in oven until golden, Fan 200, 30-40 min.

EAT with *custard*.

Sunday dinner always means a proper home-cooked pudding. Crumble is the king of puddings in our house and appears more often than any other. It's easy to make and hugely variable according to the seasons – you can crumble anything once you have mastered the basic recipe. Rhubarb crumble is my absolute favourite, but I've included this one because it was actually made by the 7yo himself, with only a little help. He collected all the produce from the allotment, made the crumble, and then wrote up this recipe himself on the computer for his 'home-school' work. If you want to make a larger crumble, make sure you multiply up the quantities – this will generously serve 2-3. For rhubarb crumble, heat 300g chopped *rhubarb*, 1tbsp *sugar*, 1tbsp *port* until just soft prior to building the crumble.

PEAR TATIN

🐦 Peel 4 *pears*, cut in quarters, remove cores.

In large frying pan, melt 50g *butter*, 50g *sugar*, add 3 *cardamom pods*, 1 *star anise*, ½ *cinnamon stick*. Heat & shake until caramelised.

Add pears, 10 min.

Cool. Arrange pears in circular tin, cut side up, point to centre.

Top with *puff pastry*, tuck in, pierce.

Bake, Fan 180, 30 min.

Turn out.

👤 I'm not a great baker, pastry maker or dessert chef and this is one of my go-to puddings. In fact, I cooked it so often, that at one point, Sam asked me not to cook it for a while because he was bored of it! However, it's fabulous, using ripe juicy pears and subtle spices. The only downside is, when you make a small version as I usually do (serves 3-4), the pears are often a little too big for the tin to make a lovely, perfect 'flower' display. I usually cut the tips off, so they fit properly. It doesn't really matter because the pudding tastes amazing however it looks. 'It all goes down the same way' – as my dad would say. Vanilla ice cream gently melting into the caramel sauce is the perfect easy accompaniment, and in fact, always makes me think of my dad, who loves a good scoop of ice cream on a hot pudding.

MICROWAVE SPONGE PUDDING

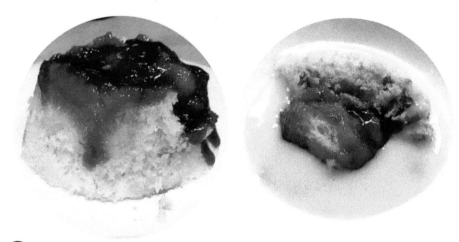

🐦 Cream 50g *butter* & 50g *caster sugar*.

Slowly add 1 *egg* & 2tbsp *milk*.

Fold in 50g *SR flour*.

Put 2 large tbsp *curd/jam/syrup* in bottom of well-greased 500 ml microwave-safe bowl.

Add sponge mix on top, cling film over.

Microwave 2 min 45 s. Turn out. Serve with *custard*.

👤 Honestly, the easiest pudding you will ever make – the one in the photograph was made from start to finish by the 7yo, except turning it out at the end. 'Daddy that pudding was awesome – it was insane'. The recipe is infinitely versatile, and you really can put anything in the bottom of the bowl – the one shown is cherry curd, but you can use *lemon curd, golden syrup, raspberry jam, honey, apple puree & blackberries*. It's a good recipe to showcase a 'hero ingredient' – a spectacularly good curd or jam really makes it special. You can store it in the fridge for a few hours once you have cling filmed it. Of every recipe that I have posted on Twitter, this is the one that most people have told me they have successfully copied.

STICKY TOFFEE PUDDING

 <u>Sponge (in mixer)</u>:
Mix 50g *butter*, 175g *dark demerara sugar*.
Add 1tbsp *golden syrup*, 2tbsp *treacle*, 2 *eggs*. 1tsp *vanilla extract*.
Add 200g *SR flour*.
Boil 200g *pitted dates* + 300ml water.
Puree, add 1tbsp *baking soda*.
Combine, mix, pour into greased 23cm square tin.
Bake, Fan 180, 45 min.

 <u>Sauce and Serve</u>:
Melt together 100g *caster sugar* & 100g *butter*.
Add 200ml *double cream*.
Boil until desired consistency & colour.
Reheat sponge portions in microwave, pour sauce over.
Serve with vanilla ice cream

A member of my research team, Buthaina, came from Saudi Arabia. Every time she went home, she brought back fabulous dates. Most of the time, I used them in sticky toffee pudding. Buthaina understood – she was herself a mum to three kids whilst completing her PhD in my lab! This is a *James Martin* recipe, who adapted it from the original inventors of the dish. The recipe serves 6-8 – you can never have too much of a good thing, and the sponge freezes.

CHERRY 'CLAFOUTIS'

Make Yorkshire Pudding batter – ½ mug *flour*, 1 *egg*, ½ mug *milk*:*water* (50:50) & a pinch *salt*.

Enrich with 15g melted *butter*, sweeten with 1 tbsp *caster sugar*.

Tip into hot *oiled* dish & drop stoned *cherries* in.

Bake, Fan 200, 30-40 min.

Serve with granulated sugar & vanilla ice cream.

This is probably the most admired recipe I have posted on Twitter – the end result is a thing of beauty, and it is just so simple. It is *not* a proper French cherry clafoutis, which is more involved and requires a sweeter, richer batter. However, having tried to do it the French way, I prefer this – it's certainly easier. When cherries are in season, this is top of my pudding list – I struggle not to eat it all.

MUM's BREAD & BUTTER PUDDING

🐦 *Butter* 6 slices *bread*, remove crusts, cut into triangles.

Put in tin, pointy bits upwards, add *sultanas*, a pinch *caster sugar* & *cinnamon* as you go.

Add 1 *egg* & 1 *egg yolk*, 1 tbsp *sugar* to 275ml *milk*. Beat.

Pour over bread, leave to soak.

Sprinkle *caster sugar* & *cinnamon*

Bake, Fan 180, 40 min.

👤 I've tried so many recipes for Bread & Butter Pudding, mostly involving making some sort of fancy custard prior to assembly. Honestly, they are a total faff and often give rubbish results. Ultimately, I went back to making it exactly the same way my Mum would have done! I wasn't disappointed – the souffled bread, with crispy bits pointing upwards, the soft custardy underneath flecked with juicy sultanas. You know it's cooked when its golden and just slightly wobbly – serve it with extra thick double cream. The 7yo ate his portion in record time and went back and stole the rest from the tin.

GRANDMA's RHUBARB DROP

🐦 Make Yorkshire Pudding batter – ½ mug *flour*, 1 *egg*, ½ mug *milk*:water (50:50), and a pinch *salt* (ideally it's just left-over from main course).

Pour into a hot oiled dish, drop in *rhubarb* chopped into 2 cm pieces.

Bake in a hot oven for 30-40 min.

Serve with lots of *granulated sugar*.

👤 I had a very special relationship with my grandma, and this recipe is the one that takes me straight back to her house. It's a poor man's version of the cherry 'clafoutis' on page 178 (which was already a poor man's version of a real cherry clafoutis). Rhubarb Drop always followed Roast Beef and Yorkshire Puddings, and the beauty of it is that you don't need to do anything special other than take your standard Yorkshire Pudding batter (make double so there is enough leftover), chop some rhubarb, drop it in and bake. That's it! Serve with *lots* of granulated sugar and I'm happy just with that. You might like some thick double cream too. Eating this, I am once again 7 years old myself, sitting at my grandma's table, enjoying the best bit of my favourite meal.

GREAT GRANDMA's SHERRY TRIFLE

🐦 For a small 17cm diameter trifle (ca. 1 litre).

Crush 6 *coconut ring biscuits*, place in bowl, spoon 35ml *Harvey's Bristol Cream sherry* over.

Cut 4 *trifle sponges* in half, generously spread *seedless raspberry jam* on cut side, put 2 layers in bowl, jam up. Spoon 65ml *sherry* over.

Make 280ml *Bird's custard* according to packet, pour over sponge when warm. Chill.

Whip 280ml *double cream* to soft peaks, spread on custard. Cling film over, leave 24 h. Top with flaked *almonds*.

👤 This is guaranteed to provoke Twitter arguments – but it's a classic family recipe that can be traced back over 100 years to my Great Grandma. Controversially, this trifle has no jelly or fruit (it has raspberry jam). Sam always said this disqualified it from being a trifle. I like to think it's more like 'English tiramisu', with silky cream and custard, and an alcohol-soaked base. You can use shop-bought custard or make your own, but my family use 'Bird's'. My Mum's recipe in the photo, handed-on to me, is for double quantities. Trifle is a serious thing in her house, and it's always made in her best (2 litre) cut-crystal bowl. The secret ingredient is those coconut ring biscuits – they make the most amazingly addictive and unique bottom layer to this trifle – and if my grandma called this a trifle, then a trifle it is!

HONEY-ROASTED FIGS and HAZELNUT ICE-CREAM

 Cut *figs* in half, drizzle with *honey*.

Roast, Fan 180, 20 min.

Toast *hazelnuts* in pan.

Mix and serve with top quality *hazelnut ice cream*.

This is pudding with absolutely no effort, perfect for a summer evening sat in the garden. It relies on two hero ingredients – the very best handmade ice cream you can find, and perfectly ripe figs. I love the combination of warm and cold, soft, and crunchy, all dripping with sweet sticky honeyed juices. I get my ice cream from Beppe at Trinacria (see page 36), who makes the best ice cream in York. I think a nut flavoured ice cream is perfect for this dish – I used hazelnut, but pistachio would also be good.

SUMMER STRAWBERRY CRUMBLE

🐦 Hull & halve 500g *strawberries*, add 1tbsp *cornflour*. Then add 30g *sugar*, 1tbsp *water*, ½tsp *vanilla extract*.

Mix 60g *flour*, 45g *rolled oats*, 80g *demerara sugar*, ½tsp *baking powder*, ½tsp *cinnamon*, pinch *salt*. Add 45g melted *butter*. Mix.

Put *strawberries* in tin, crumble topping over.

Bake, Fan 180, 30 min.

👤 We grow strawberries on the allotment, and in season there are sometimes more than even the 7yo can greedily eat while we pick them – the photograph shows Sam and the 7yo doing just that. Hunting for ways to use up strawberries, I came across this idea. In honesty, I thought it would be awful, but it was a complete revelation and was added to my list as a different, but delicious, summer pudding. In many ways, I shouldn't have been surprised, we basically love any sort of crumble in this house! This crumble cries out to be topped with good quality vanilla ice cream, rather than custard.

HONEY-ROAST APRICOTS & CARAMELISED PECANS

 Cut *apricots* in half, drizzle with *honey*.

Roast, Fan 190, 15-20 min.

Melt *brown sugar* with a little *water*, add *pecans*, stir until toasted and caramelised.

Mix and serve with the best *vanilla ice cream*.

This is another delicious, simple dessert for a hot summer's day – 20 minutes from beginning to end. You really need the best quality apricots you can possibly find. If your apricots are not so ripe, roast them for longer – they will begin to go soft and yielding. But if your apricots are really good, you don't need to push them so hard, just slightly soften them.

This recipe is super versatile, and you can easily modify the dish to add extra layers of flavour – consider adding *rosemary* or *lavender* to the roasting apricots, or perhaps a *vanilla pod* and some *thyme*, maybe *cardamom* and *saffron*. One word of warning – keep the caramelised pecans away from the 7yo, otherwise they will all be gone before you get to serve up!

BLACKBERRY RIPPLE CHEESECAKE

Process 350g *digestive biscuits*, add 120g melted *butter*. Press into greased, lined 23 cm flan ring. Fridge, 1h.

Heat 300g *blackberries*, 130g *caster sugar*, melt sugar, keep fruit as whole as possible.

Whip 350ml *double cream* to soft peaks, fold into 350g *cream cheese*.

Fold in *blackberries* for ripple effect.

Add to base. Fridge, 1h.

Decorate.

The hedgerows on our allotment grow incredible blackberries in huge numbers. In culinary terms this is great, although in gardening terms it creates a constant battle with encroaching thorn bushes. Blackberries this good really deserve to be showcased, and this is an easy, delicious no-bake cheesecake. The only requirements are fresh-picked blackberries and enough space in your fridge! Slice it up using a hot knife – this is a very soft cheesecake. I made this for a big family party, so it serves 6-8 – if you want a smaller one, simply halve quantities, and assemble it in a 16cm flan ring.

BANANA CHOCOLATE CHIP LOAF

In bowl, mash 3 *bananas*, add 75g melted *butter.*

Add 100g *sugar*, 1 beaten *egg*, 1tsp *vanilla extract*, 1tsp *baking soda*, ½tsp *salt*, 185g *plain flour*, stir until smooth.

Add 50g *choc chips* (or chopped *Reese's Minis*)

Pour in greased loaf tin, top with 30g *choc chips* (or *Reese's Minis*)

Bake, Fan 160, 50-60 min until skewer comes out clean.

One bowl, one cake tin, one hour, one cake – baking at its simplest. This is a great, straightforward recipe. Believe it or not, the banana loaf in the photograph was made from beginning to end by the 7yo (and mostly eaten by him too). They always say banana loaf should be made with old, ripe bananas, but they never seem to last that long in our house, so I usually have to buy extra, and hide them away to let them over-ripen specially, just so that we can make one of these. It's funny really, because before we adopted the 7yo – our wonderful, special, funny, caring boy – we hardly ate any bananas. Now they are in every shopping basket. For a tasty variation of this loaf cake, replace the chocolate chips with *Reese's minis* chopped into quarters – peanut and banana are a great combination.

LEMON DRIZZLE LOAF with CANDIED LEMON

 Loaf

Beat 170g *butter*, 170g *caster sugar*.
Add 3 *eggs*, mix as you go.
Add 170g *SR flour* & 1 *lemon zest*, mix.
Pour in lined loaf tin.
Bake, Fan 160, 45-50 min, or until skewer comes out clean.
Mix juice of 1 *lemon*, 60g *caster sugar*, prick warm cake all over, drizzle.

 Candied lemon

Peel 1 *lemon*, slice peel into thin strips.
Heat 100g *caster sugar* with 100ml *water*, simmer lemon peel until softened.
Drain, toss in more *sugar* to coat, leave to dry.

Lemon drizzle is my absolute favourite loaf cake – with a cup of tea absolutely nothing could be better. The candied lemon takes it to the next level, but it's a very hard job to stop the 7yo stealing it all off the top.

'YORKSHIRE PUDDING' PUDDING

🐦 Reheat *left-over Yorkshire Pudding* (page 166) in oven, Fan 160, 10 min.

Spoon *golden syrup* over top.

Eat while warm.

👤 This is a totally traditional Northern pudding, eaten after a roast dinner. If you scoff at the idea of leftover Yorkshire puddings, just make sure you bake more than you need in the first place. If you mock the very concept of syrup on a Yorkshire Pudding, then why would you put maple syrup on a pancake? I've sometimes pimped it up for the 7yo with chopped *pineapple.* We often had this at my grandma's house. Us kids would have golden syrup – it was always a battle to see who could sneak the most from the tin. Grandma preferred homemade raspberry vinegar on hers. Clearly, I'm still just a kid at heart!

CHEF KING'S LOCKDOWN DOUGHNUTS

🐦 Mix 100g *SR flour* & 50g *natural yoghurt*. Add 2tbsp *milk* to give very thick batter. Add ½tsp *vanilla extract*.

Deep fry in *oil* until golden.

Mix 25g *granulated sugar* & a shake of *cinnamon* - roll doughnuts.

Microwave *nutella* (30s) to make instant hot chocolate dipping sauce.

Eat warm!

👤 Mr King is the chef at the 7yo's school. A couple of weeks into the first Coronavirus lockdown, he posted a video of how to make homemade doughnuts from very simple ingredients. The 7yo was able to make them all by himself (obviously with careful supervision using the fryer). I honestly did not believe this recipe would work, because it is so simple – I mean aren't doughnuts supposed to be difficult, needing enriched dough and lots of proving? But, in the words of the 7yo, the doughnuts were 'SENSATIONAL'! I reckon they were better than most doughnuts you can buy from the supermarket. Hats off to Chef King – he's a legend!

RHUBARB & CUSTARD TART

🐦 Cut *puff pastry* sheet into a square, brush with beaten *egg.*

Bake, Fan 180. 20 min.

Chop 2-3 sticks *rhubarb.*

Heat till soft with 1 tbsp *sugar*, 1 tbsp *water*, ½ *lemon zest.*

Press down centre of pastry sheet and spread with warm rhubarb.

Dollop on 4-5 tbsp best-quality *ready-made cold custard.*

Swirl.

Top with *toasted almonds.*

👤 Anyone with an English allotment has a rhubarb bush quietly taking over one corner of their plot. We are no exception, and we therefore have pretty much unrestricted access to as much rhubarb as we want. Sour/sweet rhubarb and soothing vanilla custard are a classic English combination, and this is a great way of showcasing the flavours. This tart is quick, simple, and tasty – I'm really proud of this invention.

CHERRY EASY ROLY POLY

🐦 Mix 220g *SR Flour*, 110g *suet*, ca. 120ml *milk*, ½tsp *vanilla extract*. Form dough. Roll out ca. 30cm x 20cm.

Top with 4tbsp *cherry jam* leaving border.

Roll into long sausage, making sure cherries stay in roll.

Egg/milk wash, sprinkle 2tbsp *caster sugar* over.

Bake on lined baking tray, Fan 180, 35-40 min.

👤 I struggled for ages to get a jam roly poly recipe that I liked. Most require wrapping in a pleated parcel and steaming in the oven over a baking tray of water for up to an hour. Although it makes great roly poly, it is fiddly, and not very compatible with serving it as a Sunday lunch dessert. My oven is doing other stuff – I don't want it full of steam. And if I start the roly poly once everything is out of the oven, then we will be waiting an hour for pudding – trust me, the 8yo can't wait that long. This method is easy – no wrapping, no steaming. Make it in advance, then slide it into the oven 35-40 minutes before you need it. It's less of a 'steamed pudding', but on the flip side you get a sweet golden crust. The 8yo ate seconds, and asked for thirds, so it's a big win! The recipe serves 4 generously.

PASSION FRUIT CURD BRIOCHE & BUTTER PUDDING

Cut 200g *brioche loaf*.

Spread generously with *butter* & *passion fruit curd*.

Arrange in layers in baking dish adding *blueberries* as you go.

Whisk 150ml *milk*, 150ml *double cream*, 1 *egg*, 20g *caster sugar*, zest of *lemon* & 1tbsp *lemon juice*, pour in tin, soak 30 min.

Place dish in tray part-filled with water. Bake, Fan 170, 30 min.

At the time, I couldn't find a brioche loaf to make this with, but we often have leftover brioche burger buns, so I used those, which explains why the photograph isn't the prettiest! However, this is a seriously tasty Bread & Butter Pudding. Like the recipe for Mum's Bread & Butter Pudding it uses the traditional method where the custard is not made in advance, although in this case, slightly more liquid is used to soak into the brioche. It's also richer than my Mum's original recipe because it uses cream as well as milk (it is the 21st century after all, not the 1970s). Once you have got the hang of this adaptation of Bread & Butter Pudding, which is largely the replacement of bread with brioche, raisins with blueberries and the addition of lemon curd, you can imagine many more. Why not spread the bread with jam or marmalade? Why not add raspberries, or stoned cherries? Bread & Butter Pudding is your canvas – make art!

MALT LOAF and BANANA PUDDING

🐦 Cut 200g shop-bought *malt loaf* in triangles & spread with *butter*

Arrange in layers in baking dish adding sliced *banana* as you go.

Whisk 150ml *milk*, 150ml *double cream*, 1 *egg*, 20g *caster sugar*, pour in tin, soak 1 h.

Place dish in tray part-filled with water. Bake, Fan 170, 30 min.

👤 Read this recipe carefully and you will see it is a minor variation of the passion fruit curd brioche & butter pudding on the previous page, demonstrating how you can use this template recipe. Malt loaf is widely available and very cheap in the UK (the *Soreen* brand is the most famous) – it's squidgy, malty, and fruity, halfway between a bread and a cake. If you live elsewhere, try adapting the recipe with other items you can find in your local supermarket bakery. This is not the best-looking pudding once served into portions, but it tastes incredible – malt loaf and banana is just a great combination. You don't need to add any custard or cream to this one. Seconds were demanded, thirds were considered!

ICED TRIPLE GINGER DRIZZLE CAKE

🐦 Gently melt 150g *butter*, 130g *molasses sugar*, 2tbsp *black treacle*, cool briefly. Add to 110ml *milk* in large bowl.

Mix in 2 beaten *eggs* and 3 pieces chopped *stem ginger*.

Add 225g *SR flour* & 1½tsp *ground ginger*, mix.

Spoon into *buttered* & lined 20cm cake tin. Bake, Fan 140, ca. 35 min.

Cool. Prick top of cake, drizzle with 1½ tbsp *syrup* from stem ginger.

Beat 100g *unsalted butter*. Slowly add 200g icing sugar, then 1tbsp *ginger syrup* & 2tsp *lemon juice* – use to frost top of cake.

👤 Simple and delicious, this is probably my favourite cake in the world. I love the frosting using the ginger syrup and the indulgent slightly sticky texture of the cake itself, combining stem & ground ginger for maximum flavour. As you can see from the photos, the 8yo helped me make this one. Working out baking quantities is a great way of developing kids' numeracy skills. You can also see that baking is something Sam loved to do when he was very small!

BUTTERSCOTCH & BANANA HOT CROSS PUDDING

 Tear up 3 *hot cross buns.*

Thick slice 2 *bananas.*

Mix in a lined loaf tin.

Melt 50g *butter*, add 80g *dark muscovado sugar*, 225ml *double cream* & 1tsp *vanilla extract.* Bring to boil, boil for 2 min.

Pour over bun/banana mix.

Bake, Fan 180, 20-25 min.

This is a variation on a *Nigel Slater* recipe – I just tweaked the sauce to turn it into a proper butterscotch and took quite a lot of sugar and cream out. At this scale, it fills the loaf tin and serves 4-6 people – you can always scale down. This pudding is not a looker, but it's got all the flavour! It's great if you want a child-pleasing pudding for practically no effort. It might turn out of the loaf tin after cooling a little, but really you may as well just scoop it out of the tin into bowls and greedily eat it hot with vanilla ice cream or a little cold double cream. This pudding is a regular, and popular, part of our Sunday lunches. As the 8yo said while he helped me make it: "You're making this again Daddy – I love it!!"

PLUM PIE

Rub 75g *butter* into 150g *flour* to breadcrumb texture. Add 50g *icing sugar* & 1 *egg yolk*. Form dough add 1tbsp *water* if needed. Chill in cling film, 30 min.

Stone & quarter 600g *plums*. Put in 20cm pie dish with 1tbsp *caster sugar*.

Opt: add ¼tsp ground spice (choose 1 of *cinnamon*, *cloves*, *star anise*).

Roll pastry, lay over pie. Brush with beaten *egg*, sprinkle *caster sugar*.

Bake, Fan 180, 25 min.

We grow plums on our allotment – we love watching them grow from the tiniest fruit that appear as the blossoms die, through to beautiful large purple plums. This pie is just the best way to use them (apart from eating them straight from the tree). If you want a shortcut, you can buy sweet shortcrust pastry in supermarkets, but the homemade pastry really makes this pie special. Fruit pies remind me of our 2016 trip to America with the 8yo. In Shenandoah National Park, out in rural Virginia, we stayed at Skyland Lodge, and enjoyed spectacular views out over the forest from the mountaintops with dinner. We always chose a traditional American fruit pie for pudding. We adore US National Parks – in Shenandoah, one hiking trip to a remote waterfall got interrupted by a black bear – a total highlight!

CELEBRATION VANILLA CAKE

Cake

In large bowl, mix 225g *SR flour* & 2tsp *baking powder*. Then add 4 *eggs*, 225g soft *butter*, 225g *caster sugar*, ½tsp *vanilla extract* & 2tsp *milk*. Beat until smooth. (I use a stand mixer).

Spoon into two 20cm lined springform cake tins (350-400g in each). Bake, Fan 140, 30-35 min until an inserted skewer comes out clean. Leave in tins, 10 min, remove to cool.

Decoration

Slowly add 400g *icing sugar* to 200g *butter*. Mix well, then add ½tsp *vanilla extract* and ca. 2tsp *milk*.

Spread base of one cake with *raspberry jam*, base of other with buttercream. Sandwich together, buttercream cake on top.

Thinly spread top & sides of cake with buttercream.

Roll shop-bought *fondant icing*, overlay, trim base. Decorate.

This is a great recipe – it only takes about an hour, and the simple classic cake tastes fantastic (serves 12-16). To decorate, use a 20cm cake topper (as in the photo). These are edible prints you can buy online and stick to the icing – an easy way of delighting an 8yo. Alternatively, write on the iced cake with *coloured icing*, or don't ice it, just frost the top, and make a decorative pattern with *smarties*.

TOBLERONE CHEESECAKE

Crush 200g *chocolate digestive biscuits*, add 75g *melted butter*, press down in a 23cm buttered springform tin, chill.

Melt 200g *Toblerone* in bowl above pan of boiling water. Stir 200g *full fat cream cheese* until smooth. Mix the two together.

Whip 200g *double cream* to soft peaks, gently fold into chocolate.

Spoon onto biscuit base, chill. Decorate with extra *Toblerone* chunks.

Eurovision is the closest thing to a religion in this house – it's basically gay Christmas. My friends always organise parties, and they are invariably spectacular, with huge amounts of food. One year, we all took along food to represent a specific country – I drew Switzerland. Having toyed with the idea of a fondue and deciding it wasn't necessarily safe (given the large amounts of drink being consumed), I finally settled on this – a Toblerone cheesecake. By the way, this should come with a warning – there is not a single healthy ingredient in it. It is delicious though, and perfectly 'Eurovision kitsch'! You could also make a chocolate sauce to pour over it (melt 150g *dark chocolate,* 1tbsp *icing sugar,* 3tsp milk).

BLACKBERRY & LEMON TRIFLE

🐦 For a small 17cm diameter trifle (ca. 1 litre bowl).

Cut 200g *madeira cake* into cubes

Whip 350ml *double cream* with 25g *icing sugar* to soft peaks.

Crush 250g *blackberries* with 1tbsp *caster sugar* & 6 chopped *mint* leaves.

Layer the trifle: cream, cake, *lemon curd* (from jar, 50-100g), blackberries cream, cake, lemon curd (50-100g), blackberries, thick layer of cream.

Decorate with whole *blackberries*.

👤 The perfect summer trifle combining fresh blackberries from the allotment, lemon curd, sponge, and cream. This is something you can whip up quickly – it takes about 15 minutes. Like all trifles, it benefits from standing so that all the flavours come together and the cake absorbs the moisture, so leave it in the fridge for at least 2 hours. As an alcohol-free trifle, this is perfect for kids to enjoy, yet it's grown up enough for adults to appreciate as well.

BLACKBERRY & APPLE CRUMBLE TART

🐦 Peel & core 1 eating *apple*, cut into matchsticks.

Place 200g *blackberries* & the apple on a square of ready-roll *puff pastry*, leave border.

Mix 50g *flour*, 30g *rolled oats*, 60g *demerara sugar*, 40g melted *butter*. Lightly scatter over.

Brush border with beaten *egg*.

Bake, Fan 200, 25 min.

👤 A very easy pudding combining the simple pleasures of tart and crumble. Sufficiently simple that it could mostly be made by the 8yo, this was a big hit. It's perfect served with vanilla ice cream. The crumble topping here is made in the way that Americans make 'Cobbler' using melted butter – you can do the melting in the microwave to make the cooking process even more 8yo-friendly.

SCARCROFT MESS

Halve 100g *cherries* and remove stones.

Cut 4 squares *homemade fudge* (page 228) into slivers & chunks.

Toast small handful *pistachios* in dry pan, then gently crush.

Fold most of ingredients through 150 ml *double cream* that has been whipped almost to stiff peaks.

Scatter remaining ingredients over top.

Guaranteed to annoy one of my book critics who complained of my 'assembly' recipes, this is a very easy assembly pudding, and actually I'm very proud of it. It has everything you need, sweet fudge, fruity cherries, crunchy pistachios, and softly whipped cream. Satisfaction in a bowl. Fundamentally, the concept is similar to an Eton Mess, only with the sweetness of the meringue replaced by fudge, and the meringue's crunchiness provided by pistachios. I've therefore named it after our area of York – Scarcroft. The origins may be humbler than Eton, but I think it's just as good a pudding, and anyway, Etonians have been running things in the UK for far too long! You could of course use shop-bought fudge instead of homemade, but ideally, it should be slightly crystalline and not too soft. You can find my recipe for homemade fudge on page 228.

VANILLA CHRISTMAS VILLAGE

🐦 Cream 190g soft *butter*, 165g *caster sugar*, 1.5tsp *vanilla extract* with electric whisk.

Whisk in 3 *eggs*, 1 at a time.

Mix 190g *plain flour*, 1tsp heaped *baking powder*, pinch *salt*. Fold in.

Put in 1.4 litre 'Village' tin (it will rise to fill mould).

Bake, Fan 160, 30 min.

Cool, turn out. Dust with *icing sugar*.

👤 When it comes to baking, I am more interested in flavour than appearance. However, baking with a Bundt tin is such a simple way to get beautiful bakes. I bought a 'Cozy Village' tin in the sale at a local cookshop, and now the snow-dusted 'Vanilla Village' has become our new Christmas tradition – described on Twitter by no-less than *Nigella* herself as 'so lovely'! The tin is only 1.4 litre capacity, so the cake is not too big – perfect for a small family. It's so festive to have a little snow-covered village in the kitchen from Christmas Eve through till Boxing Day – even if it is gradually getting eaten by a greedy 8yo and his dad. Sam loved Christmas kitsch – he would have adored this new tradition!

A LITTLE LONGER

SPUNTINO's CRISPY PRAWN SLIDERS

 12 Brioche Slider Buns (or 6 Burger Buns)

Rub 250g *bread flour*, 20g *butter*, ¾tsp *salt*. Add 5g *instant yeast*.
Mix ½ beaten *egg*, 1tbsp *milk*, 115ml *warm water*, 1¼tbsp *caster sugar*.
Combine, knead 10 min, leave 1 h.
Shape (70g burgers, 35g sliders) on lined tray, cover, leave 1 h.
Brush with ½ beaten egg/water.
Bake, Fan 180, cup water in extra tray on oven bottom, 15 min (sliders) 25 min (burgers).

🐦 Prawns

Coat *prawns* in (i) *seasoned flour*, (ii) mix of beaten *egg*, ½tsp *Dijon mustard*, ½tsp *paprika*, (iii) *panko breadcrumbs*.
Fry in hot *oil* until golden brown all over, 2 min. Drain.
Place on sliders with crisp *lettuce*. Dress with best quality *seafood sauce*, perked up with chopped *capers, lemon & Worcester sauce*.

👤 This is adapted from a *Spuntino* recipe – one of our most-loved places. With just over twenty bar stools, around a horseshoe shaped bar on a Soho back street, opposite one of our favourite gay bars – it's the perfect place for high-end American Diner food and great drinks (the best Old Fashioned in London). Spuntino became a standard stop-off for me after science meetings in London, and I later introduced both Sam and the 7yo to its charms. The 7yo loved the little plates of food and the ability to share everything with his two daddies. Sam loved the relaxed friendly vibe, the great cooking, and the opportunity to demolish multiple cocktails in a dark corner.

One of my happiest memories is of a weekend away with Sam, with the 7yo safely at his grandparents. We installed ourselves at the counter and ate & drank our way through far too much of the menu before rolling out of the door to go and enjoy the rest of what Soho had to offer. It was just the best of times! I was properly heartbroken when Spuntino closed down this location.

This recipe is exactly the kind of thing I like to cook on a Saturday, when I have a bit more time in the kitchen, and the chance to do some baking. It works in 10-minute bursts – which is ideal for combining with childcare. Basically, it's a lazy version of the 'Prawn Po-Boy' in the *Spuntino* cookbook. Lazy because I run out of energy when it comes to the dressing (it includes raw egg, which was something Sam was not allowed to eat after his transplant because of his immuno-suppression medication).

I make the buns quite often – they can be filled with all sorts of goodies, and the larger version is an excellent way of making your burgers a bit more special. The length of time you bake the buns for depends on whether you make sliders or burgers. Sliders are perfect kid-sized food – for adults, just eat two or three! I know the recipe for them is a bit more than a single tweet but it's worth it.

'ZUNI' CHICKEN on BREAD SALAD

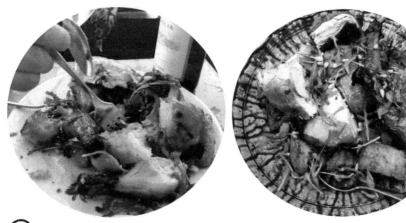

 Chicken: The day before
Season a 1.2-1.5kg *chicken* all over with 2-3 tsp *salt* and *pepper*.
Gently loosen skin on breast & thighs, stuff with *herbs* (*thyme, marjoram, rosemary,* or *sage*).
Twist & tuck wing tips behind shoulders.

 Bread Salad: As oven heats
Cut 250g *farmhouse white bread* (not sourdough) in two, remove crusts.
Brush with *olive oil*, fry to crisp & colour.
Tear into 1-3 inch chunks.
Toss with 3tbsp *olive oil*, 1tbsp *white wine vinegar*, *salt* & *pepper*.
Soak 1tbsp *currants* in 1tbsp *red wine vinegar* & 1tbsp warm *water*.

 Cooking (Total: 45-60 min).
Roast chicken, Fan 220, 30 min.
Flip onto breast, 10-20 min.
Flip back for final 5-10 min.
Toast *pine nuts*, add to bread.
Fry 2 cloves *garlic*, 4 sliced *spring onions* in *olive oil*, add to bread.
Drain *currants*, add to bread.
Put bread in baking dish, cover in foil, put in oven last 5-10 min.

 Finishing

Rest chicken.

Pour fat from tin, retain lean drippings. Add 1tbsp *water*.

Slash skin between breast & thigh, drain juice into drippings.

Warm roasting tin – stir, scrape, simmer.

Tip bread on platter, add 1tbsp pan juices, few handfuls of *rocket*.

Cut chicken in pieces, add to platter.

This is my 'Number 1' happiest food memory. Boiling the four-page recipe down into a few simple tweets is total sacrilege – I'm sorry, but I was not going to leave this dish out! I'd been at a chemistry conference in San Francisco, and Sam was with me. One lunchtime, we hopped on the streetcar and headed up towards the Castro – halfway there, we jumped off at the restaurant *Zuni*. We got a walk-in table in the bar area and ordered their famous chicken, which is a two-person sharing dish. It takes an hour to prepare, so we sat and shared a bottle of wine & some olives – the sun streaming in through the windows and the streetcars rumbling past. We chatted and laughed and just spent the best afternoon ever. And then the chicken came. Just a sublime experience – perfection that will never be matched. Sam cooked this one at home for me when we wanted to recreate the magic – you can see it in the green bowl. I haven't yet been able to face cooking or eating this dish since he died.

HAM in COCA COLA

Simmer *gammon* in *Coca Cola* (full sugar), 50-60 min/kg with 1 *onion* cut in two.

Remove skin (but not fat).

Make glaze from 1tbsp *black treacle*, 2tbsp *demerara sugar*, 2tsp *powdered mustard*.

Score ham fat, stud with *cloves*, add glaze.

Bake in foil lined tin, Fan 200, 10-15 min.

Sam loved Christmas. He loved it so much, that in his final year, he paid for his extended family to get together in a huge house in the Peak District so that we could all spend Christmas together – Christmas dinner for over 20 people. This now-classic *Nigella Lawson* recipe was one of Sam's absolute favourite things to cook (and eat). Every year we would take one to his family's Christmas Eve party. When we all got together in that final year, it was so popular, we had to go out and buy more ham and Coca Cola on Christmas Eve just so that we could make some more for the rest of the holiday. Every time I cook this now, I think of him. Twitter informs me it's also very good with ginger beer and a ginger marmalade glaze, I've always fancied trying it another way. Maybe one day, I'll move on and reinvent the tradition, but for now, making it with Coke somehow tastes like Sam.

HAM in VIMTO with CHERRY GLAZE

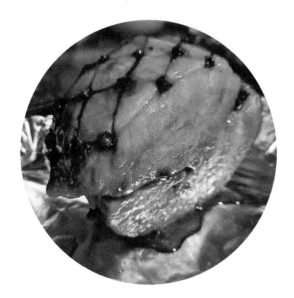

 Simmer *gammon* in *fizzy Vimto* (full sugar), 50-60 min/kg.

Heat 130g *cherry jam*, 30g *golden syrup*, 30g *demerara sugar*, ½ cinnamon stick for 3-5 min, stir well. Cool.

Put cooked ham in foil-lined tin.

Score ham fat, stud with *cloves*.

Brush ham all over with cherry glaze. Roast, fan 220, 10-15 min.

In my first book (and on the previous page), I wrote about my love for Ham in Coca Cola, but noted that I couldn't really move beyond it because it was so redolent with memories of Sam. Well, I finally did it, and Ham in Vimto with a Cherry Glaze was born! It's not that I've moved beyond Sam – I will never manage that, and nor will the 8yo. It was, however, partly the process of writing these books that helped me come to terms with my memories – organise them, collect them. Almost as if with a solid foundation of delicious food and wonderful memories, I could see a way forward. Anyway, this is easy, very tasty, and glazes the ham with a gorgeous red sheen. I suggest boiling the ham for 50 min/kg if it has been taken out of the fridge well before cooking, 60 min/kg if it is a large ham and still cold.

SAM's CHINESE BEEF CHEEK STEW (& MANGO SALSA)

Season 2 *beef cheeks*, fry in *oil* to brown.

Place beef in slow cooker (or casserole) and add 500ml *beef stock*, 3tbsp *soy sauce*, 3tbsp *Chinese rice wine* or *sake*, 2tsp *muscovado sugar*, *shiitake (or other) mushrooms*, 20g sliced *ginger*, 4 chopped *spring onions*, 2 *star anise*, pinch *cinnamon*.

Slow cook, 6-8 h. (Casserole, Fan 140, 3-4 h)

Briefly steam sliced *pak choi*, stir through stew, serve.

After I published *tw-eat*, Sam's mum sent me a WhatsApp message saying: "You may like to see this – it's the last meal Sam cooked for me. I asked him for the recipe, and he wrote it out during his last days with us. He also got Stu to make it at home for him and bring it into the hospital, but he said it 'wasn't as good as his' – ha ha!"

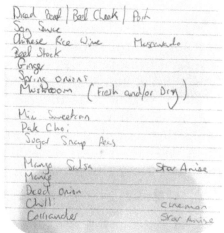

In fact, this was a dish that was massively important to Sam, possibly his signature dish, and it really should have been in Volume 1! It was something he would often cook for us on special occasions like New Year. I was delighted to rediscover it and seeing it in his own handwriting sent shivers up my spine.

The recipe uses beef cheek. If you've never had it, you must try. It responds fantastically to slow cooking, and delivers soft, tender, unctuous meat with a minimum of effort. You get a really generous portion of delicious beef. In this Asian stew the beef cheek takes on all of the fragrant flavours. Sam used to like this with mini sweetcorn, but they are something I just cannot stand – I prefer it with simple wilted pak choi – however Sam's other written suggestion of sugar snap peas is also good.

Although it's not at all Chinese, Sam liked to serve this dish with a *mango salsa* (1 *mango* peeled and chopped, 1 chopped *red chilli*, ½ *red onion* very finely chopped, juice of ½ *lime*, handful of chopped *coriander* leaves). Against the intense savoury flavours of the broth, the bright, zingy fruity flavours of this salsa lift everything – it's really very special.

The dish just needs some plain jasmine rice to finish off. A few words on cooking *rice*. I always used to boil rice in a ton of water and drain it – I was never happy with the results. One of Sam's legacies is that he taught me how to cook rice properly, and it makes a massive difference.

Rice
Rinse rice in cold water, then add just the right amount of water, a little salt, bring to boil & cover.
Immediately turn down to very low heat, then turn off completely after about 5-10 min, so water slowly absorbs for perfect fluffy rice.
For *jasmine rice*, use 1½ cups of water for 1 cup of rice.
For *basmati rice*, use 1½ cups of water for 1 cup of rice, but it benefits from soaking in water for 30 min prior to the rinsing step.
Japanese short grain (sushi) rice also needs soaking, but needs less water, so use 1¼ cups of water for 1 cup of rice.

Like many people in East Asia, I now use a rice cooker to control the heat perfectly – it's one of my favourite kitchen gadgets and takes the stress out of cooking rice.

LAMB & DATE TAGINE with FLATBREADS

 Tagine

Gently fry chopped *onion* in 10g *butter*.
Add ½tsp *ground ginger*, ¼tsp *cinnamon*, *black pepper*, 1 min.
Then add 400g diced *lamb shoulder*, brown.
Add 300ml *water*, 30g *chopped dates*, pinch *saffron*, ½tsp *salt*.
Put lid on, low heat, 90 min, top with water if needed.
Add 1tbsp *honey*, 1tbsp *lemon* juice, 100g *whole dates*, 10 min.
Serve with *flaked almonds* fried golden in butter & slivers of *preserved lemon* rind.

Flatbreads

Mix 250g *bread flour*, 250g *plain flour*, 1½tsp *salt*, 1 heaped tsp *dried yeast*.
Add 1tbsp *olive oil*, 325ml warm water, knead (I use a mixer – it's a wet dough).
Place in oiled bowl. Cover 1-2 h until risen.
Knock back. Divide into 125g pieces. (Freeze any you don't need).
On a floured surface, roll out to thin 'circles' ca. 3 mm thick.
Fry in hot dry pan, 2-3 min. When large bubbles appear and bottom side is well coloured, flip, 1-2 min.

As I mentioned earlier in the book, the first holiday I took with Sam involved a road trip through the Atlas Mountains to the

Moroccan desert. As we drove past the date palm groves, fabulous dates were being sold from the side of the road. When we arrived at our riadh on the northern fringes of the Sahara Desert, we were greeted with a wonderful lamb & date tagine. We sat together as the sun set, talking in the cool of the early evening - it felt so far from everyday life. Making this tagine transports me back there. Everywhere in Morocco, we had incredible food. There are also so many unique things to see and do - it's a hugely recommended trip if you enjoy good eating and adventure. I think it would be a fascinating family destination once the 8yo is old enough to really revel in the differences.

If you cook this tagine in a stovetop-safe casserole or tagine then the 90 min gentle heat section is better done in the oven (Fan 160), with the beginning and end of the cooking on the stovetop. Alternatively, you can put it in the slow cooker on low for 6-8 hours for this section of the cooking. If you want a 'meatier' texture, replace lamb shoulder with leg - the method remains the same. If you want more veg, throw in shredded *savoy cabbage* for the last 10 minutes with the dates. You might think it's not authentic, but when we stayed at an atmospheric riadh up in the Atlas Mountains in a restored crumbling ruin of a building, we were served cabbage tagine. We were secretly deeply unimpressed when told what was for dinner but had to eat our words - it was one of the most incredible things we ever tasted!

The flatbreads are brilliant and are a standard item in our kitchen. They go well with this tagine, but are also great with curries, stews, soups etc. There's nothing quite like tearing up warm fresh flatbread to dip in sauce. Each 125g flatbread serves one person. Once you have made a batch of dough, you can divide and freeze it - the quantities are enough to make 6 flatbreads. The dough, and concept, is *Hugh Fearnley Whittingstall's* (we use the same dough to make pizzas, see page 137). The cooking method sounds weird (raw dough in a frying pan), but trust me, it works! Once you have tried it, you will make sure you always have some dough in your freezer, and you won't ever buy vacuum packed flatbreads again. To flavour your bread, make an infused oil (e.g. gently heat crushed *garlic, rosemary* & *thyme* in *olive oil*), then tip it over the cooked bread.

HOMEMADE FISH FINGERS and 'CUSTARD'

🐦 Melt 20g *butter*, add 20g *flour*. Slowly add ca. 300ml *milk*, stirring. Add 100g grated *cheddar*, *salt*, *white pepper* and 1tsp *Dijon mustard* (optional). Simmer 5 min.

Slice 2 *cod fillets* into batons. Dip in *seasoned flour*, then beaten *egg*, then *panko breadcrumbs*.

Fry in thin layer of *sunflower oil* in pan, turning carefully until golden, ca. 5 min.

Serve with the 'custard' sauce, *peas*, and *fries/chips*.

👤 The 8yo loves Dr Who, which forms the inspiration for this dish. Famously, when the Doctor first regenerates as Matt Smith, he is starving hungry, and ransacks the kitchen of a young Amy Pond looking for something to eat. In a hilarious scene, nothing satisfies him until he alights on the combination of fish fingers and custard. In honour of that scene, which always makes the 8yo giggle, this dish was birthday tea on his 6th birthday. It was a particularly challenging birthday. Sam was extremely ill in hospital, and by this stage we all knew he was not going to recover. I had to put together something special to take the 8yo's mind off the endless string of hospital visits and the fact that everything was so uncertain. This birthday tea was crazy enough to take his mind off things and make us both laugh for an hour.

For that same birthday, he also had a trampolining party with his friends for which I made a 'Tardis' cake. Tempting as it is to include the recipe, I would not actually wish it on anyone to have to make it. Containing a spiced sponge within a decorated gingerbread shell, it took me about 6 hours of baking/decorating and would take several pages to describe. It is definitely not a '*tw-eat*' creation! However, the cake became symbolic of so much more than a birthday. I took the finished version to show Sam in his hospital bed. The cake

essentially said: "things are going to be ok… we are going to be ok… I've got this." Whatever I might have really been feeling inside, this is exactly what Sam (and the 8yo) needed to know at the time.

I love the Tardis photographs below. The 8yo and 'Jodie Whittaker' is taken in Madame Tussauds in Blackpool – one of his favourite museums in the world. The 8yo loves the Tardis – he even has an amazing Tardis wardrobe in his bedroom, created by talented friends. The other photo shows Sam as a young boy 35 years earlier, excitedly stood next to Davros. When a parent has died, links between generations take on extra resonance, they certainly help the 8yo feel closer to Sam. Some of my own most-prized childhood possessions are a Tardis & Tom Baker doll – nowadays they are collectors' items, but the 8yo loves to get them out and look at them – what good are memories if you don't use them and share them.

MAKI ROLLS

 Rice

Stand 100g *sushi rice* in water, 30 min, rinse.
Place in pan with 150ml *water* & 2tsp *mirin*. (Or in rice cooker)
Bring to boil, turn heat low, lid on, 10min. Turn heat off, 10min.
Add 20ml *rice wine vinegar*, mix gently. Put in bowl to cool.

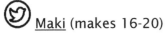 Maki (makes 16-20)

Put 1 *nori sheet*, shiny side down, on rolling mat. Cover with ½ cooled rice, leaving far long edge clear.
Lay filling (e.g. *cucumber, crabstick, carrot, tuna mayo, avocado,* cooked *asparagus,* or mixtures) lengthways, left-to-right, ⅓ way up.
Roll away from you, brush far edge with *water*, squeeze to seal.
Slice roll into maki. Repeat with second nori sheet.
Serve with *soy sauce, wasabi, pickled ginger.*

Does the 8yo love sushi? I am convinced he could eat his bodyweight in maki rolls. He can certainly eat his way through a significant portion of my salary in his favourite restaurant, *Yo Sushi*. He loves the little portions, the dipping sauces, the pickled ginger, and more than anything else, he loves the conveyor belt! Honestly, for the 8yo, the saying 'like a kid in a sweetshop' should be changed to 'like a kid in a sushi restaurant'.

In honesty, I find making sushi at home a bit of a pain – to my mind it's more of a craft than actual cooking, and I am hopeless at craft! It's something I really find quite stressful and difficult. Nonetheless, it is undoubtedly the way to the 8yo's heart, and so occasionally, making a batch of sushi rice and getting out the rolling mats and nori is a good way to spend an afternoon.

You can, of course, use *raw fish* in maki, but make sure you have a sushi-grade supplier. The best raw fish I ever ate was at my friend Jonny's house in Tokyo. His mother-in-law was Japanese; she made Sam and I the most incredible sashimi dinner to welcome us to Japan – as you can see from the photo, it was simply mind-blowing!

Making sushi is something Sam loved to do with the 8yo, it's something the 8yo's Nanny (Sam's mum) also enjoys. Sam made sure his maki were neat – to achieve this, you may need to trim the nori sheet down to avoid it 'folding in' on itself. You will also notice in the photograph there are some fancy 'inside-out' maki rolls, coated in black and white sesame seeds and with the nori tightly wrapping the filling. The batch of sushi in that photo was made by Sam with help from the 8yo (then a 5yo). Don't ask me how he did it – I have no clue. I mean, I could look it up and put it in the book, but sometimes it's just nicer to remember the man I married as some kind of sushi master rather than unmask all of the mysteries.

In fact, Sam's family are all creative and artistic – it puts me to shame. In his final year of life, Sam took up a silversmithing class. One of my most precious possessions is the silver ring that he made in the studio – I keep it on a chain and wear it round my neck whenever I want to feel him close.

UNDERTALE BUTTERSCOTCH CINNAMON PIE

 Pastry

Rub 75g *unsalted butter* into 150g *plain flour*. Mix in 50g *icing sugar*.
Add 1 *egg yolk*, 1tbsp water, form dough. Wrap in cling film, chill.
Roll pastry, line 20cm fluted pie tin, prick.
Place greaseproof paper on pastry, add baking beans.
Bake Fan 160, 20 min. Remove paper & beans, Bake Fan 190, 20 min.

 Filling

Mix 4tbsp heaped *cornflour*, 3 *egg yolks*. Slowly whisk in 450ml *milk*.
Melt 25g *butter*, add 75g *light brown sugar*, boil 3 min. Add 180g
double cream.
Slowly whisk egg/milk mix into cream/butter mix.
Add ½tsp *cinnamon*, ¾tsp *salt*, bring to boil.
Remove from heat, stir in 50g *butterscotch chips* till melted.
Pour into pie case, cool in fridge.
Stiffly whip *double cream* with a little *icing sugar*, pipe to decorate.

The 8yo adores the computer game Undertale. In the game, one
of the characters bakes you a Butterscotch Cinnamon Pie that can
restore all your health points. So, one day, I decided to make the 8yo
this as a special treat. I hacked the recipe together with ideas from
several different places and it came out really well.

Sam loved computer gaming. One of the things he used to do with the 8yo was sit and play Lego Dimensions on the PlayStation – it was a team effort, controlling the action on the screen and also using the Lego figures on the action pad to activate different characters. After Sam died, I encouraged the 8yo to play some PlayStation games. It may sound like rubbish parenting, but the problem-solving and determination required to succeed in games are good for him. It also provides worlds that he can escape to if he needs, and a space that is his, where he is the expert. Even better, in the case of the adventure game Undertale, playing it improved his reading far more than any Oxford Reading Scheme book had ever managed! I know that the 8yo sees gaming as a connection to Sam, and I think Sam would have been proud of him.

This is an American-style pie – although it sounds complicated, it's easy at heart. Make pastry, bake a pie case, make a filling, put the filling in the pie case and chill – there is no baking of the pie itself. You can make the recipe significantly easier by buying a sweet pie case from the supermarket. Then all you need to do is make the filling, pour it in and chill – you will then have your butterscotch cinnamon pie with about 15 minutes work. The butterscotch chips should completely melt into your filling – you don't want hard bits in the pie, all you are trying to do is boost the butterscotch part of the flavour profile. Some supermarkets sell butter-scotch chips, but if you are struggling to find them, bash some *butterscotch boiled sweets* (e.g. Werther's Original) until crushed into very small pieces, and stir them through the hot mixture. This pie is

surprisingly delicious, and I promise that even a small slice of it will make you feel like you have restored all of your health points.

SITGES PAELLA

Chop and fry 2 *shallots*, 2 cloves *garlic* in *olive oil*, 5 min.

Add diced small *red & green peppers* (1 of each), 5 min.

Add *squid*, 3 min.

Add 300g *paella rice*, big pinch *saffron*, 750ml *fish stock*, 1tsp *salt*.

Simmer vigorously, 6 min, do not stir, turn pan every 2 min.

Reduce heat, add (e.g.) *raw prawns*, *clams*, *mussels*, push into rice.

Cook 14 min, scatter *peas* over part way through, avoid stirring. All liquid should be adsorbed.

Turn off heat, cover, and rest 5 min. Serve with lemon wedges.

Paella was a go-to family dish – this recipe serves 3-4. It always takes me straight back to the seafront in Sitges – one of our favourite holiday destinations. Sitges is a beautiful traditional Spanish town just 30 minutes from Barcelona. It boasts some incredible food and is also an artistic and creative haven for LGBT+ people. We often went there with our gay friends from York – we would travel as a big group and just have the most wonderful time. In later years, we went there with the 7yo – he loved the sunshine, the food, and the beautiful beaches.

Every time we went to Sitges, we always had paella sat out at a seafront restaurant with a view of the water. When we took the 7yo, we ordered a big family paella and all tucked in. At the end of the meal, the waiter came over and said, 'You are not like a normal English family with fish fingers for the children – your son eats proper food with his daddies, it's beautiful'.

But perhaps my most memorable, or at least dangerous, dining experience came two years earlier, in the same restaurant, at almost the same table, with friends. It was 'Fiesta Mayor', and we settled

down for paella, knowing that the main parade may come close to the restaurant. Indeed, as the parade came down the street, we could hear the noise and see the lights. As it got closer, we realised that we were going to get front-row seats for the 'fireworks on sticks', spraying out sparks above everybody's heads. The waiters rushed round making sure the tablecloths were not going to get scorched and we sat there, plates full of paella, sparks raining down around us, music pulsing, a true moment of energy and life that fired us up ready for partying into the small hours and beyond.

Sitges really was our place, and after Sam passed away, I went back with a small group of friends for a long weekend. We scattered some of his ashes into the sea from the dramatic cliffs by the side of the church, just as the sun went down.

I haven't cooked paella since. I'm sure I will again, but it's just too resonant for me to really enjoy it yet.

LASAGNE

 Meat sauce

Finely dice & fry 1 *onion*, 1 *carrot*, 2 *celery stalks* in *olive oil*. Remove.
Fry 450g *minced beef* – as it browns, season with *salt*, *pepper*, *dried Italian herbs* & a *bay leaf*.
Add 1 glass *red wine*, reduce. Add cooked veg, can *chopped tomatoes*, ½ can *water*. Simmer 1 h, add water as needed.

 White sauce

Melt 50g *butter*, add 50g *flour*.
Slowly add 750ml *milk*, stirring to incorporate.
Add *bay leaf*, season with *salt* & *white pepper*. Simmer 10 min.

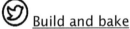 Build and bake

3 x (meat sauce, a little white sauce & *parmesan*, layer *pasta sheets*).
Top with white sauce, lots of grated *cheddar* & *parmesan*.
Bake Fan 180, 45 min (until golden).

I don't know what it is with kids and lasagne, but they all seem to absolutely love it. The 7yo is no exception - it's his favourite dinner. It's not really a single twitter recipe - be generous and think of it as three tweets. To be honest, I find making lasagne as much of a pain as trying to explain it concisely. But I really wanted to capture the template of how I do it, because when the 7yo grows up and leaves home, this will probably be the first recipe he turns to when he is feeling sad, or if he wants to impress a girl (or boy).

AFTERS

APEROL SPRITZ

 Put several *ice cubes* and an *orange slice* in a short tumbler.

Add 50ml *aperol*, slowly add 75ml *prosecco*.

Top with *soda water* to taste (Sam's taste was for minimal).

I adore this photograph of Sam, taken in the late afternoon sunshine in Trieste, Italy. I was there on business, visiting my long-time collaborator and best scientific friend, Professor Sabrina Pricl. Her and Sam got on so well – they shared a passion for good food, an unquenchable *joie de vivre*, and the love for a piece of gossip and a good story. We always planned to spend an extended period of time in Trieste, but eventually becoming dads stopped that from happening. I know there are few places Sam would rather be than somewhere in Italy, drinking an Aperol Spritz after a day exploring in the sun, while looking forward to some great food. Aperol spritz is a classic cocktail from exactly this region of North East Italy, but in recent years has increasingly become ubiquitous across the globe, to the point it barely needs a recipe. For a proper taste of *la dolce vita* with Sam, just follow the instructions above. Cheers!

STRAWBERRY GIN

🐦 Sterilise a large Kilner jar by heating in oven to 100°C.

Hull and slice 400g washed *strawberries*. Add 100g *caster sugar*. Add 700ml *London Dry Gin*.

Leave 3-4 weeks, gently inverting to mix every few days.

Strain through coffee filter into bottles for storage.

👤 My good Twitter friend Stuart Cantrill, editor of one of the leading Chemistry journals, makes amazing fruit gins. When Sam passed away, Stu sent me a collection of his work in many different flavours. Every time I drank one, I felt a little bit more healed. Inspired by his expertise, I took on the challenge of a strawberry gin. It is a fantastic summer gin and has the benefit of being super quick to make – ready to drink in less than a month. The method here can be applied to any soft fruit. You can use the same recipe for *blackberries*. In that case, you may want to add a little more sugar to taste after steeping. Although the gin can be drunk when it is decanted off the fruit, it continues to mature for 3 more months – perfect for a Christmas tipple. For sloe gin, double the sugar, and leave the gin to steep with *pricked sloes* for 3 months. That gin is ready for drinking in early spring. Pick your fruit wisely, and you can have a year-long supply of seasonal gins. Sam would have definitely approved!

SAM's MOJITO

🐦 Pour 40ml *dark rum*, 40ml *light rum*, a dash *angostura bitters*.

Add lightly 'spanked' *mint*, 1 *lime* in wedges, ½tbsp *sugar* & 'muddle'.

Add lots of *crushed ice* and top with a little *soda water* to taste.

👤 "Of all the gin joints, in all the towns, in all the world, he had to walk into mine. Play it once Sam, for old time's sake. Play it Sam. Play 'As Time Goes By'." - *Casablanca*.

Casablanca, in Sitges, was Sam's favourite bar in the world. It was a proper old-school bar, where the point of going was not just to drink, but to talk - to meet new people and forge new friendships. The irrepressible gay owners, Brandon & Juan, found unique connections between their customers and mixed the meanest cocktails in town (yes, the measures really are that large - you can always dial it back a little, but Sam would not have approved). To mark Sam's passing they invented this special mojito. We all drank to his memory and shared some of the stories that you can now find in this book, as well as many more that Sam would never want committing to print. Somehow, with his special mojito in hand I could feel him there, and I like to think that part of his spirit now drifts around his favourite haunts in Sitges, drinking, eating, and waiting for his friends to go and party with him.

7yo's BLACK CHERRY THICK SHAKE

Blend 3 scoops good *black cherry ice cream* with 300ml *milk*.

Or (if you can't find *black cherry ice cream*)...

Blend 3 scoops *vanilla ice cream*, 300ml *milk*, 250g stoned *black cherries*.

Serves 2 people topped with *squirty whipped cream* & extra *cherries*.

One of the wonderful things about food is that it helps you build new memories. The first big trip the 7yo and I made after Sam's death took us to Southern California, where I had a scientific conference. We spent several weeks holidaying first, meandering down the Californian coast from Disneyland in Anaheim to San Diego Zoo. At Crystal Cove, we stumbled across a place called *The Shake Shack*, which was just that, a shack, on top of a bluff, overlooking the sea with a fabulous view. After an idyllic morning on the beach, we had the most wonderful lunch. It was a slice of Californian perfection – I just wanted to stop time and do it every day. So now, we can make black cherry shakes at home and transport ourselves back there. The memory is ours, it's special, and it helps us look to the future, while holding on to the past.

BLACKPOOL VANILLA FUDGE

🐦 Mix 180g *caster sugar* & 50ml *milk*. Heat 2 min to dissolve

Add 160g *condensed milk*, ½ tsp *salt*.

Heat to boil. Boil/whisk 6 min Colour pale butterscotch (116-118°C)

Take off heat, add ½tsp *vanilla extract*. Whisk 1-2 min – it thickens.

Pour in lined loaf tin, rest 5-10 min, cut into ca. 18 pieces.

👤 Blackpool is one of the 8yo's favourite places in the world - the lights, the trams, the sea, the amusements, the fish & chips... and we both love the fudge shop in the photograph. When I was a boy growing up in Stockport, we visited Blackpool Illuminations every year. Despite the fact some people sneer at Blackpool, and comment on its slightly tatty edges, I have always completely loved the place – the pure escapism and fun it represents. Now, each Autumn, the 8yo and I head to Blackpool for a few days of end-of-year fun. We stay in a hotel with a sea view and make a holiday of it. We both love the fact there is so much to do – Madame Tussauds, The Sandcastle, The Tower,

The Pleasure Beach – we are never bored, and the 8yo is usually smiling. I also have an excellent track record of winning a cuddly toy on the racing camels.

This fudge brings a little taste of Blackpool back into our kitchen at home. The recipe is specifically for a small batch of fudge for a small family! It keeps in a tin for about two weeks (it gradually hardens). If you scale up the batch to use a whole can of condensed milk (400g), then you need 450g caster sugar (as you pour it out you can almost sense the onset of diabetes) and 125 ml milk. You will need to boil the mixture for a little longer – 8 minutes – check you've got the right temperature – it should be 116-118°C. You should then set the fudge in a 20cm square baking tin – it makes about 40 pieces.

Blackpool was the last family holiday we ever went on with Sam. By this stage he was really very poorly and was struggling to walk. We hopped on and off the trams, tried to keep things chilled, and managed to have an absolutely lovely time. I remember us all sitting having a drink on the end of Central Pier on a beautiful late October afternoon. The sun was setting outside the windows, and we had a view out over the Irish Sea. Our little family was all together and happy, but deep down, I knew that the sun really was setting, and that we probably would not be able to do this all together again.

RAINBOW MUFFINS with VANILLA FROSTING

 Muffins

Cream 125g *butter* with 125g *caster sugar*.
Beat in 2 *eggs*, 1 at a time, slowly adding 125g *SR flour* as you do so.
Add 1tsp *vanilla extract* and 3tbsp *milk*, mixing after each addition.
Divide into 6 bowls (ca. 75g per bowl).
Add *food colour gel* to each bowl: (i) purple (*red/blue*), (ii) *blue*, (iii) green (*blue/yellow*), (iv) *yellow*, (v) orange (*red/yellow*), (vi) *red*.
In 8 muffin cases load & gently spread 1 heaped tsp of each coloured mix from (i)-(vi) in order.
Bake, Fan 180, 15-20 min.

 Frosting

Beat 60g *butter*, 1 min. Add 1 tsp *vanilla extract*. Mix in 120g *icing sugar* in portions, and then add 2-3tsp *milk*. Beat until fluffy. Pipe onto muffins.

Finally, I come properly to one of the happiest days of my life – the day back in 2010 when I married Sam. We had a beautiful time with friends and family at *The Hospitium* in Museum Gardens, York. The sun shone, the sky was blue, and everything was right with the world. The most memorable food item was our cake. Long before rainbow cake was 'a thing' we decided we wanted a wedding cake with an ordinary exterior, but a rainbow interior – just like us. The first cake-maker we asked thought it was too difficult, the second was not interested in making a cake for a gay ceremony. Eventually, we found a wonderful local cake-maker, who embraced our vision. The rainbow cake has since become a baking classic, almost a cliché, but back then, it made the cutting of our cake a landmark moment.

This recipe remakes the idea of a rainbow cake in cupcake form. It's an easy bake, and fun to do with kids. However, be warned, it uses a lot of bowls, and loading the batter into the muffin cases gets messy. If you want layers, very gently spread each batter with the back of your teaspoon as you load it. If you want something more abstract just load the batter in splodges. First time I tried this, I used liquid food colours, but they bleached out to muddy brown during the bake. Use extra strong gel colours designed for baking! You can buy every colour of the rainbow, but there's something fun about blending your own - if you have red, yellow, and blue, you can mix the others.

Museum Gardens is a very special place for us. As well as having been married there, the 'Edible Wood' in the Gardens, which showcases edible plants, is the location of Sam's memorial bench. We scattered some of his ashes there and visit regularly. The 8yo loves exploring the gardens, and we often take something to eat and sit on Sam's bench for a while.

Some people think the story of our family is sad - that we have been unlucky. Others say Sam was lucky to have had us both. In fact, it was the 8yo and I who were lucky. Our lives are so much richer for having had Sam in them - anyone who knew him would understand. Things may have been hard, but it's far better to have had something remarkable than to have never had it at all. As I hope these books show, memory gives us strength and sustains us. As we reinvent memory into new traditions, like these rainbow muffins, the 8yo and I look to the future with optimism and togetherness.

INDEX

CPSIA information can be obtained
at www.ICGtesting.com
Printed in the USA
BVHW022255021221
623077BV00005B/501

9 781739 967000